CW01025360

THE FORGOTTEN
TUDOR ROYAL

THE FORGOTTEN TUDOR ROYAL

MARGARET DOUGLAS, GRANDMOTHER TO KING JAMES VI & I

BEVERLEY ADAMS

PEN & SWORD
HISTORY

AN IMPRINT OF PEN & SWORD BOOKS LTD.
YORKSHIRE – PHILADELPHIA

First published in Great Britain in 2023 by
PEN AND SWORD HISTORY
An imprint of
Pen & Sword Books Ltd
Yorkshire – Philadelphia

ISBN 978 1 39908 590 8

Typeset in Times New Roman 12/16 by
SJmagic DESIGN SERVICES, India.
Printed and bound in the UK by CPI Group (UK) Ltd.

Pen & Sword Books Limited incorporates the imprints of Atlas, Archaeology,
Aviation, Discovery, Family History, Fiction, History, Maritime, Military,
Military Classics, Politics, Select, Transport, True Crime, Air World, Frontline
Publishing, Leo Cooper, Remember When, Seaforth Publishing, The Praetorian
Press, Wharncliffe Local History, Wharncliffe Transport, Wharncliffe True Crime
and White Owl.

For a complete list of Pen & Sword titles please contact
PEN & SWORD BOOKS LIMITED
47 Church Street, Barnsley, South Yorkshire, S70 2AS, England
E-mail: enquiries@pen-and-sword.co.uk
Website: www.pen-and-sword.co.uk

Or
PEN AND SWORD BOOKS
1950 Lawrence Rd, Havertown, PA 19083, USA
E-mail: Uspen-and-sword@casematepublishers.com
Website: www.penandswordbooks.com

Contents

Acknowledgements

There are many names that are synonymous with the Tudor age, we all learnt about King Henry VIII and his Six Wives, Bloody Mary and the Virgin Queen Elizabeth, but what of those whose lives have been forgotten? It has always been important to me that women's stories from history do not get lost among those of others, and Lady Margaret Douglas's story became one of these. She was an integral part of Tudor life, living in a time of religious turmoil; I wanted to know what it was that made her the beloved niece of King Henry VIII, confidante to her cousin Queen Mary, and enemy of Queen Elizabeth.

I would like to thank my publisher Pen & Sword, especially Jonathan Wright for allowing me the opportunity to write about Margaret's extraordinary life and Charlotte Mitchell for all her support throughout the writing process and to Laura Hirst for all her encouragement. I would also like to thank Karyn Burnham for her her kind words during the edits.

As always, thanks to my family, Mum, Dad, Chris, Paul, Alison, Mary, Danni and Faith. My friends, Emma Powell, Kathryn Baxendale, Lorraine Mawdsley, Leona Steel, Chris Smith and Marie Drelincourt.

Thank you to all the wonderful historians that have gone before me and have provided a wealth of material that I was able to draw upon. Also, thanks to the Royal Collection Trust for granting me permission to use their images.

Finally, thanks go to Margaret herself for never being afraid, always being headstrong and for living a life full of ambition and intrigue at a time when religion and gender restricted the lives of women.

Tudor Timeline of Events

22 August 1485   Henry Tudor defeats King Richard III at the Battle of Bosworth to become king of England.

18 January 1486   Henry VII marries Elizabeth of York uniting the Houses of Lancaster and York.

28 November 1489   Birth of Margaret Tudor, Queen of Scotland.

1489   Birth of Archibald Douglas, 6th Earl of Angus.

28 June 1491   Birth of King Henry VIII.

18 March 1496   Birth of Mary Tudor, Duchess of Suffolk.

1502   The signing of the Treaty of Perpetual Peace between England and Scotland.

1503   King James IV of Scotland marries Margaret Tudor.

21 April 1509   King Henry VII dies, King Henry VIII becomes King of England.

11 June 1509   King Henry VIII marries Katherine of Aragon.

10 April 1512   Birth of King James V of Scotland.

9 September 1513   Death of King James IV at the battle of Flodden Field, his son succeeds him as King James V of Scotland.

6 August 1514   Queen dowager Margaret Tudor marries Archibald Douglas, 6th Earl of Angus.

7 October 1515	Birth of Lady Margaret Douglas at Harbottle Castle, England.
18 February 1516	Birth of Queen Mary I.
21 September 1516	Birth of Matthew Stewart, 4th Earl of Lennox.
1519	Birth of Henry Fitzroy, Duke of Richmond & Somerset.
1528	Margaret's parents Archibald Douglas, Earl of Angus and the dowager Queen Margaret divorce, she goes on to marry Henry Stewart.
1530	Death of Cardinal Wolsey.
1530	Margaret arrives at the court of her uncle, King Henry VIII of England.
14 November 1532	King Henry VIII secretly marries Anne Boleyn.
23 May 1533	Archbishop Cranmer declares the marriage between Queen Katherine of Aragon and King Henry VIII null and void.
7 September 1533	Birth of Queen Elizabeth I.
19 May 1536	Queen Anne Boleyn executed at the Tower of London.
30 May 1536	King Henry VIII marries Jane Seymour.
23 July 1536	Death of Henry Fitzroy, Duke of Richmond & Somerset.
July 1536	Lady Margaret Douglas and Thomas Howard are imprisoned in the Tower of London for entering a marriage contract without the monarch's approval.

12 October 1537	Birth of King Edward VI, his mother Queen Jane Seymour dies shortly after the birth.
October 1537	Lady Margaret Douglas is released from the Tower and removed to Syon Abbey; Thomas Howard dies shortly after her release.
6 January 1540	King Henry VIII marries Anne of Cleves, the marriage is dissolved six months later.
28 July 1540	King Henry VIII marries Catherine Howard.
1542	Lady Margaret Douglas is in disgrace again following a dalliance with Charles Howard, she is sent to Kenninghall as punishment.
13 February 1542	Queen Catherine Howard is executed at the Tower of London.
8 December 1542	Birth of Mary, Queen of Scots, she succeeds to the Scottish throne at just six days old following the death of her father King James V following the Battle of Solway Moss.
1 July 1543	The signing of the Treaty of Greenwich between England and Scotland.
12 July 1543	King Henry VIII marries Katherine Parr.
December 1543– March 1551	The Rough Wooing in Scotland, a series of invasions of Scotland by England.
29 June 1544	Lady Margaret Douglas marries Matthew Stewart, Earl of Lennox at St James's Palace.
1546	Birth of Henry Stewart, Lord Darnley.
28 January 1547	Death of King Henry VIII, he is succeeded by his son King Edward VI.

10 September 1547	The Battle of Pinkie Cleugh.
6 July 1553	Death of King Edward VI, he is succeeded by his half-sister Queen Mary I, following a failed coup of nine days by Lady Jane Grey.
25 July 1554	Queen Mary I marries Philip of Spain.
May 1557	Birth of Charles Stewart.
17 November 1558	Death of Queen Mary I, she is succeeded by her half-sister Queen Elizabeth I.
1562–3	Margaret is placed under house arrest at Sheen Palace and Lennox at the Tower of London for plotting the marriage of their son, Lord Darnley to Mary, Queen of Scots.
29 July 1565	Marriage between Lord Darnley and Mary, Queen of Scots at the Palace of Holyroodhouse, Edinburgh.
1565–7	Margaret is arrested and sent to the Tower of London following the marriage of Lord Darnley to Mary, Queen of Scots.
19 June 1566	Birth of King James VI of Scotland (later King James I of England).
9–10 February 1567	Lord Darnley is murdered at Kirk o' Field, Edinburgh.
2–16 May 1568	Mary, Queen of Scots escapes from her prison on Loch Levan and flees to England.
4 September 1571	Death of Matthew Stewart, Earl of Lennox, he is assassinated while in his role as Regent of Scotland.

1574–5	Margaret and Bess of Hardwick plot to bring about a marriage between Charles Stewart and Elizabeth Cavendish. Margaret is sent to the Tower of London as a result.
1575	Birth of Arbella Stuart.
7 March 1578	Death of Margaret Douglas, Countess of Lennox aged 62, at her home in Hackney. She is buried in Westminster Abbey following a state funeral.
8 February 1587	Mary, Queen of Scots is executed at Fotheringhay Castle.
24 March 1603	Death of Queen Elizabeth I, she is succeeded by Margaret's grandson King James VI of Scotland who becomes James I of England at which point the Stuart age in England begins.

Introduction

The role of women in any era has always been a battle against the patriarchy and this was no different in Tudor England or Stewart Scotland. Throughout the reign of King Henry VIII women had been be viewed as no more than vessels to bear an all-important male heir, even a queen could be displaced if she did not give birth to a living son and heir and this so-called failure was seen as a fault on her part and her part alone – which of course is nonsense. Queen Katherine of Aragon fought bravely against her husband's wish to cast her aside for a younger lady called Anne Boleyn who it was hoped would be more successful in bearing a male child. It was deemed, in the eyes of the king, that the reason Katherine had only provided him with a surviving daughter, the Princess Mary, was that she had been previously married to his elder brother Prince Arthur. When Arthur died, Henry took Katherine as his bride and Queen, but when it became apparent that she was not going to provide him with a living son, all of a sudden, this union was a sin and the marriage ought to be made null and void, leaving Henry free to marry again. Katherine had given birth to a boy, named Henry, on 1 January 1511 but sadly he died within weeks of his birth leaving the couple devastated. Henry saw this as punishment; he felt the lack of a legitimate son was God's proof that he was displeased with the marriage. This was further compounded when his mistress Elizabeth Blount gave birth to a healthy boy in 1519.

This became the foundation for his 'Great Matter', he wanted a divorce from Katherine in order to marry Anne Boleyn, but when she eventually became Queen in 1533, she fared no better and was only able to give Henry one living child – another daughter, named

Princess Elizabeth. Soon enough, the king was looking for a way out of his second marriage so he could try his luck with someone else. But there would be no divorce for Queen Anne, when Henry decided her time was up, he had her arrested and executed. She was beheaded in the grounds of the Tower of London on 19 May 1536 on a trumped-up charge of adultery and treason. Of course, her real offence had been her failure to provide Henry with a prince, which in reality caused the king to grow bored of her. The final straw came when Anne miscarried a son, a child that would have saved her from her fate. During Anne's final pregnancy Henry paid court to one of her maids of honour, Jane Seymour. It is suggested Anne miscarried after she found the pair together, causing her to fly into a rage and lose her child.

At what point Henry decided he wanted to make Jane his new queen is not clear but it was more than likely three months prior to Anne's arrest and execution. He knew he could not divorce Anne without then having to acknowledge Katherine was his true wife and queen, so her execution became the only course of action he could take, for this he engaged the services of Thomas Cromwell who schemed to give Henry his wish. Finally, in 1537, Queen Jane fulfilled the king's wish and gave birth to a healthy boy who was named Prince Edward, after his lothario grandfather King Edward IV. For Jane, the glory did not last long; she died from complications just twelve days after the birth leaving Henry devasted and the newborn prince without a mother. Henry's fourth wife, Anne of Cleves, was swiftly moved aside as she did not resemble the beauty painted by Hans Holbein, and Catherine Howard was to suffer the same tragic fate as Anne Boleyn. Katherine Parr managed to outlive Henry but even she was hounded by men over religion and nearly lost her head for it.

North of the border in Scotland women did not fare much better. Henry's elder sister Margaret Tudor had been married at just 13 years old in 1503 to King James IV of Scotland, although she did not join her bridegroom until months later when she was of childbearing age. It took until 1507 before her first child was born, it was a boy, but he sadly died just after his first birthday. Her next two pregnancies also ended with infant death but her fourth pregnancy produced a healthy baby boy, the heir to the throne of Scotland, the future King James V. Margaret then gave birth to another boy, Alexander, Duke of Ross, just after the death of her husband. Margaret would go on to give birth again, to a daughter by her second husband, the Earl of Angus, she would go on to call her Margaret.

So, it was against this backdrop that Lady Margaret Douglas was born in 1515. Her birth was traumatic, her mother had been hounded out of the country by men who struggled to accept she had chosen to marry as she wished, thereby denying them the opportunity. The Scottish lords would have looked to use her to forge an alliance with a foreign power; she was seen as an asset rather than a woman who had already done her duty to the country by providing them with a king. Women of Margaret Tudor's rank were merely pawns in the marriage market, they were to be used for the benefit of their family or to improve dynastic relations and very few had a say in the matter. Margaret's younger sister Mary would feel the anger of their brother Henry when she married Charles Brandon against his wishes. Henry had married his beautiful younger sister to the aged king of France, but when he died shortly after the marriage she felt it was her time to marry for love. Henry fined the couple to such an extent they could no longer afford to reside at court.

Boys were important for the continuation of the line but girls had their uses too, they could be married far and wide in an attempt to create an all-important foreign alliance. Many a young princess had been sacrificed in the marriage market by her father, brother or uncle in the hope she would bring with her wealth and power. Sometimes these marriages turned out to be miserable for the women, if she was trapped in a loveless marriage there was absolutely nothing she could do about it, but there were some marriages that turned out to be true love matches.

Lady Margaret Douglas would be one of these royal women, she would grow into a fierce and feisty woman who held sway with her equally fierce and feisty uncle, King Henry VIII. There were not many people who escaped his wrath once they had incurred his displeasure, but there was something about Margaret that protected her, whether that was her royal blood or her personality we do not know. She also enjoyed an equal marriage with her husband Matthew Stewart, Earl of Lennox, it was a happy union that produced the all-important heir and spare; sadly, it also experienced profound loss, with the death of six of their children before they left infancy.

Margaret's was a life lived at full pelt; she was ambitious – not just for herself, but her family too. She was a woman that had a strong sense of her place in the world and used her position of power to try and better the fortunes of those she loved, she may not have always succeeded but that did not matter, her sense of what was right mattered and she stuck to those principles regardless. This was particularly true when it came to religion. Living through a time of great religious change, Margaret remained a devout Catholic, even when those around her were converting to Protestantism she remained steadfast in her faith showing true courage and determination, even if it meant feeling the displeasure of her cousins Edward VI and Elizabeth I.

Margaret was never more passionate than when she was advancing the fortunes of her children; her eldest surviving son, Lord Darnley, would experience the very heights of power – she was even willing to serve time in prison for the benefit of her children. This behaviour shows us a woman who was brave enough to defy conventions of the time, at a time when queens were beheaded, she somehow managed to dodge the axeman despite pushing the boundaries of royal protocol on more than one occasion.

Lady Margaret Douglas, Countess of Lennox, was the daughter and cousin to queens, a niece, granddaughter and half-sister to kings, but above all that she was a woman who never shied away from danger. She was brave, courageous – and at times, reckless. She fought for what she believed was her birthright and instilled that belief in her children. Whether she ever really harboured hopes of gaining the throne for herself we do not know, but in her children and grandchildren she saw a vision of a United Kingdom of England and

Scotland, and she was willing to risk imprisonment in order to see the realisation come true. She had Scottish and English noble blood flowing through her veins which placed her at the forefront of royal life in both countries, and she also held important roles at the English court for most of her adult life.

She was well respected and liked by many on both sides of the border all her life, a life which was played out during the one of the country's most turbulent times; when queens lost their heads and kings died young Margaret Douglas, Countess of Lennox, remained steadfast and lived through it all. She led a remarkable life and this is her story.

Chapter 1

Origins and Birth

Margaret Tudor, queen dowager of Scotland, mother of King James V of Scotland and daughter of King Henry VII of England, took flight under starlight from Linlithgow Palace. She was heavily pregnant with her seventh child and was heading for the English border and the safety of the realm of her brother, King Henry VIII.

It was 1515 and Scotland was in the midst of upheaval; their monarch, King James V, was a child aged just 3 years old. His mother had been declared regent following the death of her husband King James IV at the battle of Flodden in September 1513; his forces had been routed by the English and he was slain on the battlefield. The queen dowager was eventually removed from her role as regent and as guardian of her two sons following her ill-advised marriage to the ever-ambitious, handsome and dashing Archibald Douglas, 6th Earl of Angus, on 14 August 1514 at the parish church in Kinnoull, Perth.

The Douglas clan is an ancient family in Scotland that fractured into the Black Douglas and the Red Douglas clans. Angus was the head of the much-disliked Red Douglas clan and he somehow managed to convince Margaret he was in love with her and that marrying him would offer her and her sons the level of protection she would need to keep a firm grasp on her power, but it all went disastrously wrong. Following the death of James IV, the Scots seemed more than happy to support the deceased king's wishes and acknowledge her role as regent for her son, taking the view that her brother was a powerful enemy and one they did not want to anger. But as soon as they got wind of the Angus marriage, they began to distrust the queen and were concerned that any union with him, who was considered one of the country's prominent peers, would make them too powerful.

When it was discovered the couple had wed the council requested she appear before them to explain her actions. She obliged and they informed her that by remarrying she had violated the terms of her deceased husband's will and so had forfeited the right to be regent and guardian. In a move to further undermine her position, the council also advised her that she could no longer use the title of queen; going forward she was to be known as My Lady, the King's Mother.

In one swoop she had lost the respect of the council and lost control of her children. The council needed to act so they invited John Stewart, 2nd Duke of Albany, to become regent in Margaret's place. He had been living in France for some time and was popular at the French court so was reluctant to return to Scotland, but as the king's second cousin he was his closest male relative and was persuaded to return to take control. The terms of James IV's will also stipulated that the queen would lose custody of her children should she remarry; he wanted her to remain unmarried so the young king would not be influenced by a nobleman who was power-hungry. When Albany arrived, he went to Stirling Castle to seize the royal brothers. The queen was understandably desperate to protect her young sons, her thoughts must have turned to her uncles: King Edward VI and his brother Richard, Duke of York; they had been taken to the Tower of London, supposedly for their own safety by someone who was supposed to protect them, only for them never to been seen again. Margaret initially held out against Albany and his forces, she stood holding her sons' hands on the ramparts of Stirling Castle and refused point blank to hand them over, but eventually realised she had no choice; reluctantly, she gave over the welfare of her two young sons to Albany and retired to Edinburgh Castle where she signed the deeds confirming she had passed the guardianship to the new regent. This must have been heart-wrenching for the young mother, being forced to hand over her two surviving sons having already lost children to infant death. But she did not have time to dwell on her situation for she was pregnant again and requested permission to leave Edinburgh to travel to Linlithgow to await the birth. This was her seventh pregnancy; she was aged just twenty-five.

Understandably she did not want to stay under the watchful eye of Albany, and she somehow managed to convince the nobles she would be much more comfortable giving birth in the majestic Linlithgow Palace as was the custom for many a royal Scottish birth. Linlithgow offered peace and solitude, it stands beside the loch on a low hill and new royal apartments had been added by James IV in 1513 making it a more modern and comfortable residence. Permission was granted and she left Edinburgh with Angus, on the pretext that she was going to enter confinement upon her arrival. The truth is, she never entered her confinement chamber; she was convinced her life was at risk and felt she had no option but to flee, for the safety of her unborn child. They rode out of Linlithgow just two days after their arrival, under the cover of darkness at midnight on 13 September 1515.

Accompanied by Angus's brother George Douglas and a handful of servants, they fled south in the direction of the English border. Margaret rode hard clutching her swollen belly as she did so – she was in the latter stages of her pregnancy so this journey would not have been easy on her, one can only assume she felt so sure of the danger she faced that she was compelled to undertake it at any cost. The fleeing party had agreed to meet Alexander, Lord Home, just outside the town of Linlithgow and from there he was to take them south to Blackadder Tower via Tantallon Castle, Angus's impregnable fortress overlooking the Firth of Forth. Tantallon sat high upon the cliff top on the East Lothian coast overlooking the Bass Rock, which sits out in the Forth. Built in the fourteenth century by William Douglas it would be his son that would eventually inherit the castle and become the 1st Earl of Angus. It made sense for them to travel here, it had withstood many bombardments in its past and would offer security should they need it. It would also give Margaret some much needed rest, but they must have known they did not have long before they were being chased down.

It did not take long for word of the escape to reach the ears of Albany and the council; he sent a force of men to track them down and bring them back to Edinburgh. He wanted Margaret in Scotland where he could keep an eye on her, she had powerful relations and Albany was fearful she would return to Scotland with the force of an English army behind her. In retaliation of her flight and refusal to return, Albany confiscated anything that he felt belonged to the crown, including jewels, gowns and plate. The Scots did not want anything of value going to England where it could be lost or sold.

Angus was known for being predominantly pro-English which made him unpopular with many Scottish lords, it was felt his presence among the group would encourage them to attack. Worried that Tantallon would be the first place they would be sought, they continued on to Blackadder Tower; it was important for Margaret to take regular rest so they stayed a short time before moving on towards the border and the safety of Berwick. Unfortunately, the English governor of the town, Sir Anthony Ughtred, had received no authority to receive Margaret and her party, leaving them with no option but to turn back and make the daring trip back across the border and west to Coldstream Priory where they sought comfort and shelter. The fact they were not expected in England gives a clear indication that Margaret had not sought prior approval from Henry to enter his country. She either expected it not to be an issue, or the escape from Linlithgow had been a short time in the planning. Despite being an English-born princess, she was also a queen of Scotland, with a Scottish husband and a young son who now sat upon its throne. Ughtred's cautiousness is understandable but the retreat back into Scotland must have been a terrifying ordeal, knowing they were being tracked down and could be taken at any moment. Margaret wrote to Henry from Coldstream pleading for help, but they were like sitting ducks and had to endure an agonising wait before instructions arrived from the English court.

Thankfully, Thomas, Lord Dacre, Henry's Warden of the Northern Border Marches and long-time supporter of Margaret's, arrived at Coldstream Priory with good news. He managed to get there before the Scots came with their offers of peace. He was to accompany Margaret, an English princess by birth, home to England. But Henry had certain demands; while he was happy to accommodate his sister, he stipulated that no Scottish man or woman was to accompany her over the border. He did not want Scottish people in his realm causing trouble and trying to influence his sister, who had shown thus far that she was easily swayed by Angus when it came to making important decisions. This meant Margaret had to proceed without any of her Scottish escort – and without her husband; although he may have breathed a sigh of relief at this, she was more than likely devastated. She faced the daunting prospect of giving birth without any assistance from women she knew; we do not know who offered Margaret assistance during the birth but can assume they were local women known to Dacre and his wife. As she ventured forward on her journey into England and to safety, the others turned back towards Scotland and an uncertain welcome. Queen Margaret crossed the border into England on Sunday 30 September 1515, she was finally safe knowing Henry would protect her and her unborn child.

Dacre had been ordered to escort Margaret to his official residence, Morpeth Castle, but in her condition and with her time getting closer he felt it would be safer to take her to the nearby fortress of Harbottle Castle in the unsettled region of Northumberland. Given its remote location, Harbottle Castle offered the security needed; border raids were commonplace and with the tension in the region constantly riding high an attack was to be expected at any time. It was highly unlikely the Scots would attack Margaret on English soil, or make any attempt to lure her back – to do so would be a huge political error as it would goad Henry into striking back with the full force of his army. Harbottle Castle was built in the twelfth century and sits on the banks of the River Coquet. At the time of Margaret's stay it was in a dilapidated state thanks to many attacks from Scottish border raiders, although at the time Dacre had more trouble controlling the English than the Scots. The castle was often used as a prison making it inadequate for any birth, let alone a royal one, but Margaret desperately needed rest so the small travelling party headed for Harbottle. Dacre considered it was not worth taking any risks with Margaret's safety; the wellbeing of mother and child was of the utmost importance. No doubt Henry had impressed upon him just how illustrious his guests were and the last thing he would have wanted was to fail his monarch or his sister.

The decision was made for Margaret to remain at Harbottle until after the birth of her baby, she was due in four weeks and they would not have wanted to linger at Harbottle any longer than was necessary. But Margaret's labour pains started two weeks early. She laboured in agony for nearly forty-eight hours, her screams could be heard throughout the castle and no doubt across the wild remote Northumbrian hills. The birth was arduous and Margaret suffered greatly; there were genuine concerns that mother and baby might not survive the ordeal, but finally, on 7 October 1515, she delivered a healthy baby girl who she named Margaret.

For someone who had given birth to a king in the luxurious surroundings of Linlithgow Palace, a birth like this would have brought home to Margaret the dire straits she was now in, and with a newborn to consider, her next move would have to be well calculated. Margaret found she had two choices. She could either turn north and return to Scotland in the hope that Albany would treat her kindly, the outward signs were that he was ready to negotiate terms that would be favourable to Margaret where she could be reunited with her sons. She knew Albany had been heavily criticised across the European royal courts for his behaviour towards her; people were shocked that he had forced her to flee the country in terror while heavily pregnant, so he was ready to welcome her home to save his reputation.

Alternatively, she could turn south towards London and hope her brother would welcome her and her newborn daughter to his court. Dacre urged her to travel to London, knowing the trouble this could cause Albany.

It was against this tumultuous backdrop that Lady Margaret Douglas was born. Her brother sat on the throne in Scotland but as he was only a child himself, he was powerless to offer his sister and their mother the protection needed to return safely. Albany could not be trusted to keep to his promises, for all the queen knew he could have her arrested the second she stepped over the border. Meanwhile, her uncle sat on the throne of England and he was powerful with great wealth and could offer protection to them both.

This little baby, whose cries echoed around the castle, had no option but to hope her mother would make the right decision, but the birth left Margaret vulnerable both physically and mentally and her road to recovery was going to be long and hard. Thankfully, she had Dacre and his family to offer her guidance and comfort, and the knowledge that Henry was ready and willing to welcome her home to London.

Chapter 2

The Early Years

Margaret wrote to Albany to remind him of the reasons she fled and to announce, 'I am delivered and have a Christian soul, being a young lady.' The baby may have been a longed-for daughter for her mother, but as a girl there was not the usual fanfare that would have accompanied the birth of a boy. So insignificant was Margaret's birth deemed to be, that it took Lord Dacre ten days to write to King Henry to tell him the good news that his sister had been safely delivered of a girl and that he had a niece; no doubt that would have been a much more hastily written letter had the baby proved to be a boy. Regardless of the sex Henry was pleased to hear he was an uncle and requested the nobility in the surrounding area pay homage to his sister and niece.

But Dacre had been wrong to dismiss the importance of this little girl, for at the time of her birth her uncle was childless and the fact she was born on English soil meant she was one of his subjects and had a very legitimate claim to the English throne. Any claim she had superseded that of her older Scottish-born half-brother James, for at this time English law did not acknowledge any claim to their throne from someone born outside the realm. In fact, at the time of her birth young Margaret stood behind only her mother in the line of succession and would remain there until Katherine of Aragon gave birth to a surviving child. But little Margaret was lucky; she had been born to an English princess in an English castle rather than to a Scottish Queen in Scotland; if she had been born just five kilometres to the north in Scotland, her life would have taken a completely different turn. She may have had a Scottish father, but due to the circumstances of her birth, she was a person of significance to the

English and would remain so for the rest of her life. Did her mother realise, as she fled across the border, that she may be about to give birth to a future monarch of England? All for the sake of a few miles, Margaret's future would now follow a different path.

Margaret was christened in the chapel at Harbottle Castle the day after her birth on the 8 October; as was custom for the time, the ceremony would probably have been attended by Dacre and her godparents, but her mother would not have been in attendance. Her godfather was the recently appointed Cardinal Thomas Wolsey, Henry VIII's chief advisor (by proxy), indicating once again the importance of her personage and of the respect shown to her mother – although Wolsey might have been chosen for the role without his prior consent in the knowledge that he would be a willing godfather.

The royal party finally left Harbottle Castle on 26 November 1515 and travelled the short distance south to the more comfortable surroundings of Morpeth Castle, they arrived by early December and spent a lavish Christmas as the guests of Lord Dacre and his family. Dacre had been good to Margaret since her arrival in England, he offered her comfort and reassurance at what must have been a terrifying time for her and he was determined she would not miss out on all the Christmas fun. There was much merriment that Christmas amid what had been a terrible ordeal; although Margaret had hoped to spend the festive season with Henry and his court, she was not well enough to travel that distance. Instead, Henry sent Sir Christopher Garneys, one of his gentlemen ushers of the king's chamber, to Morpeth with expensive gifts for his sister and niece, including gowns of cloth of gold, shifts and undergarments, as well as rich tapestries and plate all of which delighted her, he also reiterated his wish that they will visit him when she was well enough to do so. Margaret was eternally grateful to her brother for sending her such luxury and commented: 'Here you can see that my brother the king has not forgotten me, and that he will not let me die for a lack of clothes.' Henry understood that as a Tudor his sister would have wanted to display her royal status and, as a young woman, Margaret liked to do this through fine clothes and jewels. It would have hurt her immensely to have left all her finery in Scotland, but thanks to Henry her regal status was being restored.

But the fine clothes and exquisite jewels could not hide the physical pain she was in. Garneys wrote to Henry with an update and commented that his sister was 'one of the lowest brought ladies with her great pain of sickness, that I have seen'. He then goes on to describe her ailments: 'Her grace hath such a pain in her right leg that this three weeks she may not endure to sit up while her bed is a-making.' The letter goes on to say: 'when her grace is removed it would pity any man's heart to hear the shrieks and cries that her grace giveth'. It makes for grim reading; poor Margaret was undoubtedly in agony but knowing that her brother had not forgotten her brought huge comfort, and while she remained on good terms with him, she stood a good chance of being able to return to Scotland to win back her regency and her sons.

The pain described in Garneys's letter was a result of the agonising sciatic pains Margaret suffered in the weeks following the birth, which made her recovery long and difficult; it had probably been caused by long hours in the saddle fleeing from Linlithgow while heavily pregnant. She had to be carried about in a chair and was often heard to be screaming out in pain, spending much of her time bedridden and unable to move about on her own. What effect this had when it came to bonding with her new baby we do not know, but physically it must have impeded Margaret's ability to hold her newborn daughter, while mentally the level of pain must have clouded her mind. Dacre was so concerned over the queen's health that he wrote to Henry requesting the royal doctor be sent direct from London because the local physicians had failed to ease her discomfort, Henry readily obliged but it would take until the end of January before Margaret began to recover her strength.

Margaret was to face a further setback when she discovered her beloved 20-month-old son, Alexander, The Duke of Ross, her favourite child, had died unexpectedly on 18 December. Garneys wrote in his letter to Henry that there were genuine concerns that 'if it came to her knowledge, it would be fatal to her' – a sentiment that was shared by Dacre. He felt that at this stage in her recovery Margaret was in no state to receive this news, so he held back the information until March when he deemed her strong enough to learn the grim news; naturally, she was devastated and could not control her outpouring of grief. Dacre grew concerned and once more requested the royal physician attend her; again, it was hoped this tragedy would not put her recovery back too far.

The young prince of Scots' death at Stirling was sudden; the cause is not recorded but, in a time when many children died in infancy, it was not entirely unexpected. In her grief, Margaret, egged on by Henry, instantly laid the blame on Albany for her son's death, she also raised concerns for the welfare of the young King, worried he would follow the same fate as his younger brother. Comparisons were quickly made between Albany and Richard III, who at that time was blamed for the death of his nephews in the Tower of London in order to usurp the English throne. Was Albany planning to do away with the young Scottish King so he could place himself on the throne? It is highly unlikely, but all the same he was desperate in his attempts to convince everyone of his innocence over the death, and in his treatment of the young prince's mother. In his mind his treatment of Margaret had been acceptable, after all it was her that had broken the terms of her husband's will; the Scottish nobles had been more than accommodating to her in the role of regent for her son, which showed they were willing to accept her rule. But Henry was unhappy with the treatment of his sister at Albany's hands and continued to accuse the regent of being heavy handed and forcing her to part from her children, stealing her jewels and giving her no option but to flee for her life in the late stages of pregnancy. There was talk that Henry would avenge the treatment of his sister and the death of his nephew by waging war against Scotland.

As far as Albany was concerned, it had all been a misunderstanding. He claimed he had never forced Margaret to flee and had made many pleas for her to come home, offering to negotiate good terms for her return. Was Albany right, had she overreacted? It is impossible for us to put ourselves in Margaret's shoes the moment she faced Albany in the courtyard of Stirling Castle, when she placed her sons' little hands in his not knowing when, or indeed if, she would ever see them again. She could not let that happen to her unborn child, although they had no jurisdiction to remove this child from her care, she was blinded by fear and took the only option she felt was available to her as a young widow. In her mind it was no longer safe for her to remain in Scotland and, backed by Angus, flight was her only option.

Nevertheless, Albany was urged to make peace with Margaret, not just to stave off rumours of wrongdoing but to hold off an English attack. It was perceived by the Scots that Margaret had the full force of an English army at her disposal, whether this would have ever come to pass we will not know; Henry VIII was not averse to war with his neighbours north of the border, but whether would he have put his army at his sister's disposal is questionable. On 24 January 1502, as part of the negotiations for Margaret's marriage, Henry VII and James IV had agreed to the Treaty of Perpetual Peace at Richmond Palace. The aim of the treaty was to bring an end to the warfare that had blighted England and Scotland for over 200 years, particularly in the border region that was constantly being fought over. Sadly, the treaty was broken in 1513 when James declared war on England; he did so in defence of France, who held the much earlier Auld Alliance with Scotland, signed by both countries in 1295 when they agreed to unite against England.

Henry VIII was just as keen to reignite the wars, he was not the peacekeeping monarch his father had been and was often on the lookout to cause trouble with his neighbours in the north. As per the terms of the treaty, James was excommunicated by Pope Leo X; James would later die in the retaliation attack by the English at Flodden. Margaret had been sent north by her father in the hope that her union would bring peace between the countries and now suddenly, she was back on English soil with a wayward husband and a newborn baby, having left Scotland under a cloud of suspicion.

Shortly after their arrival at Morpeth news reached Margaret that Henry had lifted his ban on Scottish visitors, which meant she and Angus could be reunited and he could finally meet his newborn daughter. The happiness was short lived however; Angus declared he was not willing to travel to London, as it was his wish to return to Scotland to reclaim his lost lands. He told his wife he wanted to make peace with Albany and had been working for some time to achieve this. This was betrayal of the highest order as far as Margaret was concerned. Angus turned his back on his wife and daughter and left them behind in England to return home, where he was eventually pardoned by Albany. His estates were returned to him along with Margaret's – as her husband he had a right to them, but his callous behaviour left his wife and child with very little income. He had not even had the courtesy to say goodbye to Margaret; just two weeks after learning of Ross's death, she found herself abandoned by her husband.

Disgusted by Angus's behaviour and treatment of his wife, the ever-trustworthy Dacre chased Angus as far as Coldstream in an attempt to get him to change his mind but he was unsuccessful and returned to Morpeth to be greeted by a much-maligned Margaret. What was not clear at the time was that Angus was not just returning to Scotland for his lands; he quickly became reacquainted with Janet Stewart of Traquair, his love before he made an advantageous marriage to the queen. The couple lived at Newark Castle, one of the queen's own residences, and Janet soon gave birth to their daughter.

Feeling hurt and abandoned, Queen Margaret pressed ahead with her plans to travel to London. Eventually departing Morpeth Castle with her daughter on 8 April 1516, they began the long journey south where she would finally be reunited with her brother. They travelled via Newcastle where she bid a tearful farewell to Dacre, he had been with her since she stepped over the border and it must have given him much joy and relief to finally see her on her way home to London. It was then on to Durham where she was greeted by Sir Thomas Parr, father to the future Queen Katherine, from here she was escorted by

Henry Percy, Earl of Northumberland, as far south as York. On the 27 April the queen's party arrived at Stony Stratford and from there they headed to Elsynge Palace, just north of London. Finally, on 4 May, after a journey of just over four weeks, the travelling party arrived at Bruce Castle in Tottenham, north London. The house was owned by Sir William Compton, a member of Henry's court, and he made it available for the two siblings to be reunited. Following an absence of thirteen years from the English court, Queen dowager Margaret of Scotland finally came face to face with her brother King Henry VIII. The last time they had seen each other Henry was just 12 years old, now he was a handsome, athletic 25-year-old king with an imposing presence who had sat securely on his throne for seven years. When Margaret placed her baby daughter in his arms, he lifted her up and called her Marget, an affectionate name that would stick and the loving bond between uncle and niece was formed in that moment. Margaret must have been an enchanting baby to behold, she captured her uncle's heart, no doubt with a toothless grin, and in him she had her protector.

The royal party stayed just two days at Bruce Castle before making the journey on to Baynard's Castle in the City of London before formally joining the court at Greenwich where Margaret and Henry were joined by their only surviving younger sister Mary, Duchess of Suffolk, former queen of France. The arrival of Margaret was greeted with much joy and celebration; Queen Katherine, who had recently given birth to the couple's first healthy child, Princess Mary, was delighted to meet her sister-in-law. Nestled in the loving bosom of her family after so long must have been a wonderful feeling for Margaret; she had finally come home and, despite her aching loss for little Alexander and the pain of separation from young James, she must have felt contented for the first time in many months.

It was the first time in many years the Tudor siblings had been together, and Henry honoured the occasion by hosting luxurious banquets and jousting competitions. But the arrival of his sister and niece at his court placed Henry in a difficult position. While he understood her predicament and sympathised with her situation, the young Scottish king was his nearest male heir and at the point of their arrival there was great tension between England and Scotland. Margaret was much more valuable to her brother in Scotland where she would be in a better position to try to influence her young son in an attempt to bend him to England's will. Henry was going to have to strike the right balance between political diplomacy and sibling loyalty, but for the time being Margaret could relax under his care and recover from her travails. The English court was happy and relieved to have its princess safely home.

While it would be politically beneficial for the queen to return to Scotland, there was much sympathy at the English court for her situation. Albany was detested and widely condemned for his treatment of the queen dowager and her young daughter, but safely ensconced in her brother's court and reassured of his support, Margaret could look to the future and plan how she would become reinstated as the regent for her son. In the meantime, Margaret and her daughter settled at Great Scotland Yard; the residence held for the rare visits of Scottish monarchs just a stone's throw from Whitehall – convenient for visiting the court. At this time Great Scotland Yard was a large comfortable residence and would have given Margaret the opportunity to build her own household, it would be their home for the next eleven months. During that time Margaret would enjoy the company of her sister Mary and her infant son Henry, and her sister-in-law Katherine of Aragon and her newborn daughter, Princess Mary. While their mothers talked all three babies joined each other in the royal nursery and it must have made a very satisfying sight. The three queens and their young children formed a happy social circle and for a time, Margaret was happy; gone for the time being was fear and constant worry, replaced by contentment and relief.

Margaret must have known they could not impose on Henry's generosity for too long, he had a country to run and she had a son she had not seen for nearly two years. But Margaret was suffering financially, she was out of pocket to the tune of thousands thanks to her callous husband who had misappropriated her rents; she had not had the use of her clothing, jewels and the other trappings of her royal lifestyle as it was all in Scotland in the care of Albany. She had received just a fraction of the revenues owed to her and was desperate for money; conscious of how much Henry had done for her she had no option but to turn to Wolsey for a loan. Henry was starting to become weary of his sister's constant demands for money, he met the cost for their upkeep as well as their household. She owed everything to her brother's kind generosity but he did not have bottomless pockets and soon enough it became apparent to Margaret that she and her daughter were going to have to return to Scotland. Margaret was physically and mentally stronger now than when she had arrived and felt able to fight for her son and her financial rights.

It was time to face Angus again but her return was a diplomatic minefield; certain terms needed to be agreed upon before she would even contemplate leaving the comfort and security of London. First, she wanted to be restored as guardian for her son and second, she wanted her revenues returned to her. The young king agreed and assurances were made, she received her permission to travel and made plans to leave.

It did take some urging on Henry's part, but by May 1517 Queen Margaret and her 18-month-old daughter departed London and set out on their return north to Scotland. Henry assured his sister that he would not abandon her and was ready to defend her if needed; bolstered by this she turned her attentions back to home and to Scotland, she had been away too long and the time had come to return and forge a new life for her and her daughter. The journey was the reverse of the one they had made just over a year before; accompanied by George Talbot, Earl of Shrewsbury, they travelled up the Great North Road but when they reached Doncaster the queen fell ill and had to rest for a short while. From there they rode on to York where they were met once again by the Earl of Northumberland, he escorted them up to Durham and then on to Berwick. Along the route many of England's noble gentlemen came to pay homage to the king's sister, she was treated with deference wherever she stayed but it must have been a bittersweet experience for her, she was having to leave the elegance and formality of the English court behind and return to a country that threatened her liberty.

It took just under a month to reach the border, but on 15 June 1517 Margaret and her daughter crossed over into Scotland, the young Margaret's first visit to her father's homeland. They had initially been met at Berwick by Albany's deputy and he escorted them over the border, they were then met at Lamberton Kirk by Angus, his cousin the Earl of Morton, and other important dignitaries. Despite all her concerns and worries, Margaret was pleased to finally be reunited with her husband, although it made for an awkward reunion for Angus. He had not seen his wife or daughter for over a year and had to be coerced into making the trip to greet them, he quite clearly did not relish the idea of Margaret being back in Scotland where his comfortable life was about to be exposed. It would have been more convenient for him if his wife had stayed in England – he could have continued to live on her revenues with Janet Stewart and their children without scrutiny, but with Margaret's return that suddenly became threatened. One can only imagine what Janet Stewart thought of her lover's new circumstances. Of course, she was aware he was married to the queen, but in England she was a distant problem that did not require too much thought; now she was back in Scotland there was a very real issue to face. For Janet there was the distinct reality she could see herself and children usurped – if Angus was forced to return to his wife where would that leave them?

Albany had assured Margaret that the welcome would be warm and that all her finery would be returned to her and her funds paid in full, but there was a catch: she must acknowledge she would not be able to return to her former status of queen or as guardian to her son. When she returned to Edinburgh, she was given her old apartments at Holyrood but it soon became clear she was not going to be restored as guardian to James or given any role of importance; Margaret must have wondered what she was doing in a realm that had no place for her, she may have been the king's mother but that counted for very little if she was denied access to him. Sadly, things were going to get worse when she discovered Angus's duplicity.

All this formed the backdrop to the young Margaret's childhood; thankfully, at such a young age she would not have understood that her circumstances were somewhat compromised. She had gone from the luxury of the English palaces, where she had young cousins to play with and where she was doted on and admired, to the tense atmosphere of her parents' broken marriage where no one took much notice of her. She was the infant English daughter of the queen dowager and as such she held no position of importance in Scotland, but that did not mean she was immune to the tumultuous events that were going on around her, that would one day shape her outlook on life.

Chapter 3

An Unhappy Homecoming

It would soon become clear to Queen Margaret that her husband had been living openly with his mistress, but worse still was the realisation that he had been betrothed to Janet before his marriage to her, potentially making their marriage invalid. It also became apparent to Margaret that the funds from her own estates had been keeping them in a life of luxury and they had even been living in one of her properties. It was not uncommon for a noble man to take a mistress but he would usually ensure his wife and child were financially taken care of, but in Angus's case he seems to have been willing enough to let them struggle for money, forcing them to live on the generosity of others.

From that moment on Margaret must have known her marriage was over – although it had never really got going and appeared to have been doomed from the very start. As a couple they had spent more time apart than in each other's company, and when Angus returned to Scotland instead of accompanying his wife to London, Margaret should have realised all was not well. It is clear that Angus never truly loved his wife; to him she was nothing more than a means of gaining power and once he saw that plan was not going to work, he turned his coat and abandoned her without a second thought. His continuing refusal to reconcile dashed any last remaining hope Margaret had for rebuilding her fractured marriage, and any affection she may have still had for Angus soon evaporated leaving the Lady Margaret Douglas in a precarious position.

The young Margaret's movements around this time are sketchy to say the least, she all but disappears from the records. There are those who believe that Angus took Margaret to Tantallon when she was 3 years old, where she was given her own household and raised in the status of princess – after all she was his legitimate heir and he was well within his rights to do this. But this seems unlikely given her young age, Angus was many things but I do not believe he was the kind of man to take a young child from her mother's care, given that up to this point father and daughter barely knew each other. That is not to say he had no involvement in his daughter's upbringing and that she did not visit him at Tantallon, but to take full custody of her seems unlikely. Therefore, we assume Lady Margaret was permitted to stay in the care of her mother, although her involvement with her daughter would have been limited. Although a queen would not have been concerned with the day-to-day upbringing of her children, that would have been left to nurses and household staff, Margaret would have kept her daughter close, for there was no provision for her to have her own household so she more than likely travelled with her mother between her residences. To Angus, it seemed pointless in disrupting his daughter, particularly as he was in favour with Albany and therefore, happy to live an easy life.

The decision to leave her with her mother may also come from a place of guilt, knowing the wrongs he had done her since they married, but he does not seem the kind of man that would hold on to guilty feelings. It is more likely that he did not want the extra financial burden of her upkeep, despite being more than capable of providing for her.

The running of Scotland was about to change when Albany returned to France at some point in 1517 to care for his ailing French wife – he was married to his first cousin Anne de la Tour, Countess of d'Auvergne, and having spent much of his life in France he very much saw himself as a Frenchman. With Albany gone, Margaret had fresh hope of being able to regain a foothold in the politics of Scotland but she would have to bide her time and wait for the right opportunity to present itself. On 26 August 1517, along with the Duke of Alencon, Albany signed the Treaty of Rouen which sealed the renewal of the 'Auld Alliance' between Scotland and France. A part of this treaty was the promise of a French bride for the Scottish king, this news would not have gone down well in England and Henry would have been disappointed that Margaret could not prevent it from happening but it would appear Queen Margaret held no sway when it came to political issues, or matters to do with her son.

The king was only 5 years old when the treaty was signed so there were no immediate plans for a proposal but he would eventually go on to marry two French brides. His first wife was Madeleine de Valois, the daughter of King Francois I, who was initially concerned that the Scottish climate would damage her already fragile health so declined James's request to marry her, but James was smitten and persevered. Francois eventually relented and the couple were married at Notre Dame Cathedral in Paris on 1 January 1537. Madeleine travelled to Scotland as queen in May, arriving at Leith on 19 May 1537. Sadly, she died from tuberculosis at Holyrood on 7 July, aged just 16. This had been a true love match for James; he had previously been contracted to Mary of Bourbon, daughter to the Duke of Vendome, but declined that proposal when he fell in love with Madeleine. Following her death James married Marie de Guise in 1538, she came from one of France's most powerful families and would give birth to James's only legitimate heir, Mary. Margaret never met her first sister-in-law but we do know she met Marie de Guise in London.

Scotland needed a new regent and so turned to a first cousin of James IV, James Hamilton, 1st Earl of Arran. He was selected to lead the council of regency in Albany's absence and soon became bitter enemies of the Douglas clan due to the execution of Lord Home, Arran's brother-in-law. Home had been against Albany's appointment as regent from day one and the pair never saw eye to eye. Albany requested that Lord Home meet with him to iron out their differences, Home agreed to the meeting but was arrested and taken to Edinburgh Castle as Arran's prisoner. Somehow Home managed to persuade Arran to let him escape; Arran agreed, trusting that Home would keep the peace, but as soon as he was free he attacked Dunbar Castle. His freedom did not last long after the attack, Albany managed to convince him all was forgiven and invited Home to Holyrood. Thinking he was in favour, Home went with his brother but was arrested upon his arrival. They were both thrown into prison and Home was accused of allowing the murder of James IV at Flodden, which seems a far-fetched idea; in the end both he and his brother were charged with treason and beheaded. Home had been a staunch ally of the Douglas clan, he even accompanied Margaret on her escape to England. His execution meant Angus would remain at loggerheads with Arran throughout much of Margaret Douglas's life.

With Arran now acting as regent, the queen's access to her son was severely restricted and without a husband at her side it became increasingly easy for Arran to dismiss her, isolating her from government even more. If she wanted any communication with her son, the queen knew she had to act – and fast, otherwise she would be swept aside in all matters concerning the welfare of James and the country. It was time for Margaret to play Angus at his own game and knowing of the animosity between the two men, she saw an opportunity to ally herself with the regent. In the process she would use Arran as a means to reclaim some authority and to help her claim back her revenues from Angus. Arran welcomed Margaret into his fold and had some success in trying to reclaim some of the money that was owed to her, but the request that Angus and his mistress vacate her properties was met with stern rebuffs; as her husband, by law all her property belonged to him to use as he wished and there was little she or Arran could do about it.

Knowing her marriage was all but over Margaret set about officially separating from Angus, talk of divorce was rife and when the news reached Henry down in England he claimed to be disillusioned by Margaret's plans. He urged to her to return to him as divorce was considered a sin and she had no valid reason to leave him – adultery on the part of the man was acceptable. Henry would not apply the same rules to his own marriage when fell in love with Anne Boleyn and wanted an annulment from Katherine. Maybe what Henry failed to realise was that Angus had no love for his sister – he was happily ensconced in her castle with his mistress; it was clear that Henry's previous offer of help did not extend to her marital woes. In reality, Margaret had very little to offer Angus, she had no power and no love and he already had her money; the only thing they had in common was their daughter, who must have looked on in anguish as her parents split became more acrimonious. Margaret stuck to her plan and would not be persuaded otherwise; knowing she was at odds with her brother must have caused her some distress but she was left with no choice other than to turn yet further in the direction of Arran, who was more than happy to fight her battles if it meant an opportunity to cause the Douglas clan trouble.

In the middle of all this trouble and strife was a 3-year-old girl; young Margaret remained with her mother and was more than likely shielded from the worst of the fighting between her parents. It had perhaps not yet dawned on Angus just how important his little daughter could be in terms of dynastic opportunities and what she could potentially bring him. The truth of the matter is we do not have a lot of information about Margaret at this stage in her life, but we can make some assumptions based on her rank and the experiences of her mother at the same age. Having been brought up a princess, her mother would have ensured she was given the education befitting her rank and station. Being a Tudor meant Queen Margaret was well aware of her royal status and what that meant in terms of what would be expected of her. She had been told from a young age that she would marry a prince or king of a great nation and that her duty would be to provide her husband with a well-run household and children, and no doubt she would have impressed these lessons on her daughter. Margaret would have made sure her daughter understood who she was and what she was entitled to, a lesson Lady Margaret would put to good use when fighting for her own son's rights years later. We can speculate how much of her Tudor lineage Margaret was taught over her Scottish one, but it's likely Lady Margaret would have had a good understanding that her relatives south of the border in England were wealthy and powerful. Her mother also trained her to be God-fearing, graceful and virtuous, all of these lessons would prove to be valuable to Margaret throughout her life.

In 1519 there was to be a brief reconciliation between Margaret and Angus, encouraged by Henry and members of the Douglas clan; she was willing to overlook the desertion, but the adultery proved to be a step too far. Publicly, all appeared to be well, but behind closed doors the resentment was still apparent. Angus knew it was important for him to remain in Henry's good books during his ongoing battles with Arran but he refused to give up his mistress and to cease misappropriating his wife's funds and property; by the end of 1519, they had separated again. This time it was to last, and she quickly returned to Arran's fold once more.

Over the next couple of years Angus continued to cause trouble and unrest in Scotland, so much so that when Albany returned to regain the regency in 1521, he found his power lessened even further. Margaret decided to align herself with Albany in a bid to keep her husband from having any control. Peace in Scotland was a fine balancing act but Angus was always on the lookout for trouble and when he attempted to undermine Albany's rule, a charge of treason was brought against him which led to his estates being confiscated and the sentence of death placed on him. Surprisingly, Margaret interjected on his behalf and the sentence was commuted to exile in France. The hope was that without Angus meddling, the country could return to some form of normality and peace.

Again, there is speculation regarding Margaret's whereabouts; there are discussions around the idea that Angus took her with him to France but that seems unlikely as he would not have wanted the burden of providing the care required by a young girl, but there are no clear records to confirm her exact movements. Angus stayed in France until 1524 at which point, he received an invitation to travel to London from his brother-in-law, King Henry, much to Margaret's annoyance. This proved too much for her to bear, she decided she no longer wanted any connection with Angus and with the help of Albany petitioned Pope Leo X for an annulment to their disastrous marriage on the grounds of adultery and his prior betrothal to Janet Stewart. This was a risky move to make, given it could cause problems on various levels. Henry had made his feelings clear on the matter of her separation from Angus, many of Scotland's nobles urged her to rethink, as it could potentially render Lady Margaret illegitimate, lessening her importance in the marriage market. Margaret would have to make it clear that she was not aware of any pre-contract on Angus and that she married him in good faith if she was to save her daughter from the stain of illegitimacy. It also risked damaging relations with England. Henry and his queen, Katharine of Aragon, along with Cardinal Wolsey, were against her plans, the thought scandalised the English court; Henry claimed she had brought dishonour on herself and they urged her yet again to reconsider but this time she was determined to see her separation through.

While her parents' marriage was crumbling, Margaret was likely still in the care of her mother in Scotland. As a young girl at court, the daughter of a queen no less, her education was important. Margaret would have spoken Scots dialect and may have been educated in French and Latin and would have picked up English from her mother. She would have been expected to make a very good marriage and therefore, would need to know how to manage a large estate with a great household; she would also need to be trained in accomplishments such as singing, dancing and playing various musical instruments such as the lute and virginals. When she was old enough, she would also have been instructed in how to ride, and hunt using falconry, this part of her education would more than likely have come from her father because the Tantallon hawks are well known and Angus even commented on his daughter's skill in the saddle, going as far as saying she was more accomplished that many men he knew. Her education would have followed a very similar pattern to that of her mother's when she was growing up at her father's court in England. Margaret's mother, Elizabeth of York, tried to be as involved as she could in her children's upbringing, despite them having their own household at Eltham Palace; the queen visited them regularly for updates on their progress and made suggestions if she felt certain areas needed attending to. This would have been passed down to Margaret and she in turn passed it on to her daughter. Young girls may not have been as important as male heirs in terms of ruling the country but they still had an important dynastic role to fulfil and making sure she was well equipped for a life as a wife to a leading noble at court was important.

In 1524 Margaret petitioned the Scottish estates to dissolve the regency under Albany as she felt the king was now old enough to reign in his own right – he was 12 years old. The parliament agreed and the Regency was dissolved. With the help of Arran, Margaret moved the young king to Stirling where she was recognised as his chief advisor. The country was in complete disarray, it was a lawless land where no one knew who to trust and it was this that the queen faced when she was restored to power. In the October of 1524 Henry granted Angus leave to return to Scotland, he wanted a pro-English influence in Scotland and Angus was more than happy to oblige Henry, he seized the opportunity to grab power back and returned home to take control of the young king. When he arrived though he found Margaret was in power and wanted nothing to do with him, there was no chance she was going to let Angus take control of anything and when he arrived in Edinburgh, she turned the cannon of the castle on him. By Margaret's side was Henry Stewart and it was rumoured that they were conducting an adulterous affair. He was eleven years younger than Margaret and he supported her in her quest to have Angus removed. Angus was angry and retreated back to Tantallon but that was not the end of the matter and Margaret was put under pressure to give her husband a place on the council; she relented, and in February 1525 Angus was ready to make his move. Lady Margaret's feelings are not recorded at this point, she was just 9 years old and may not have been fully aware of the constitutional crisis engulfing the country, she may have had an inclination that her parents were at the centre of the troubles but would more than likely have been protected by her nurses from learning the details.

A fragile peace was formed between Margaret and her husband after the decision was made to create a council of four nobles, to each of whom the king's wellbeing would be entrusted for a fixed period of time. Angus was allotted guardianship of the king from July until November, at which time he was to pass it over to the next person. When the November came, he refused to release the king, effectively holding him prisoner for the next three years. There were attempts to free him from Angus's clutches, including a daring attempt by John Stewart, 3rd Earl of Lennox, who bore down on Edinburgh with 10,000 men under his command; he was defeated at the Battle of Linlithgow Bridge in the August and died shortly after. Angus went on to claim Stirling. The attack failed and so the king remained under Angus's power, during which time he managed to control Scottish government by exploiting his position, he wielded power through the young king, appointing many members of the Douglas clan to prominent positions of power. What Angus was thinking is anyone's guess; of course, he was power hungry but he must have realised when the king reached his full majority, he would want his revenge. The actions taken by Angus at this stage resulted in James learning to despise him, his house, and the English; the impact this would have on Lady Margaret would change her life forever.

In 1525 the 10-year-old Margaret received her first marriage proposal, it came from James Stewart, Earl of Moray, the illegitimate son on James IV and sixteen years older than Margaret. The queen backed this proposal as she wanted to make sure Margaret married one of her (the queen's) supporters and not Angus's. The last thing the queen wanted was for Margaret to marry a Douglas relative that would turn her against her mother. Angus firmly declined the match with Moray and over the next three years he was to enjoy great power in Scotland, managing to silence Margaret and her supporters in the process.

In March 1527, Pope Clement VII finally granted Queen Margaret a divorce from her adulterous husband but when Angus heard the news, he was furious. She had always been a source of power and wealth and now that was threatened he became angry and volatile; he was further incensed when he learnt she was to remarry, and in retaliation he forced the king to ride to Stirling to lay siege to the newlyweds. Margaret and Henry Stewart, son of Lord Avondale, had been conducting an affair for some time and they married on 3 March 1528, Angus was not pleased to have been usurped from his lucrative posts by a relatively minor nobody. Despite his attempts to turn the king against his mother and new stepfather, King James actually supported the match and created Stewart Lord Methven, much to his mother's delight. Unfortunately, England did not approve of the marriage, Henry bombarded his sister with letters urging her not to commit adultery and to reconcile with Angus. He was desperate for Margaret to redeem her soul for it would be damned if she continued down such a ruinous path. Queen Katherine and Cardinal Wolsey once again both urged Margaret to reconsider, for the sake of her daughter if not for herself. The Pope agreed that Lady Margaret's legitimacy should not be tainted by her parent's divorce, he was satisfied that Queen Margaret knew nothing of the pre-contract between Angus and Janet Stewart and therefore, declared she had made the marriage in good faith. Much to Margaret's relief this meant her daughter was born in wedlock in the eyes of the church, and so was legitimate. Many urged Angus to remarry quickly and have sons that could inherit his titles and estates. At one time Margaret would have been upset if she thought she had offended her brother, but now she was married and her son was close to his majority his words did not have the same impact on her – and as Henry was pursuing his own divorce his words were nothing short of hypocrisy in his sister's eyes.

When King James reached the age of 16 in April 1528, he knew his time for freedom had finally come. He quietly bided his time and waited for the perfect opportunity to make his escape. That moment came in the June of that year during a hunting trip in the grounds of Falkland Palace. He, along with accomplices, managed to give Angus the slip, making their escape on horseback. The king fled straight to his mother and Methven who welcomed him with open arms at Stirling Castle, he was now old enough to take the full reins of power on his own and one of his first duties was to deal with his enemies. He banished Angus from Scotland and warned that no member of the Douglas clan should come within seven miles of his person, the only exception to this would be his younger half sister, Margaret. He wanted revenge but so did Angus, and that revenge would change the life of 12-year-old Lady Margaret Douglas and would set her on a path to England.

Chapter 4

Arrival at the Tudor Court

Angry at his former wife, Angus decided to remove the young Margaret from her mother's care. In December 1527, he demanded Margaret hand over their daughter to him at Stirling Castle and for the second time in her life Margaret was forced to part with her child in front of the castle gates. Whether he did this as an act of revenge on his former wife or through concern for his daughter we do not know, but given his fury over her remarriage and his hatred of her new husband we can assume it came from a place of anger and resentment. We also do not have a clear understanding of what Lady Margaret's relationship was like with her father. There is no indication of how much time she had spent with him nor what her thoughts or wishes were, but she seems to have gone willingly with her father for there is no record of any skirmish and neither does it appear that James interceded on his mother's behalf. In the eyes of the law Margaret belonged to her father and he had every right to remove her from her mother's care, regardless of the king's orders. It is hard to gauge what kind of relationship mother and daughter shared, the queen does not come across as being particularly maternal with Margaret, as much of her focus was placed on her son, but queens were not overly involved in the lives of their children anyway. There is such scant information relating to Margaret's childhood, it would be unfair to suggest her mother was anything other than loving and that she was no doubt distressed at their parting. There is, however, strong evidence to suggest they never saw each other again despite attempts being made to recover her from Angus's clutches.

Angus took Margaret to his fortress at Tantallon where she would be cared for by his cousin's wife, Isobel Hoppar. Isobel was the daughter of a successful merchant in Edinburgh and thanks to her vast wealth she was considered a powerful political figure in Edinburgh. Following the death of her first husband she married Archibald Douglas of Kilspindie, which brought her into Margaret's life. Isobel was often described as a headstrong, ambitious and domineering woman who had too much influence over the men in her family. She was even accused of having such a negative influence on Angus, many believed he would have been better received in Scotland had it not been for Isobel Hoppar. Isobel would have taken care of Margaret's immediate needs; she would have continued to train and educate her and it would be her influence that helped shape the adult Margaret.

Following his removal of Margaret from her mother, Angus was once again named a traitor by King James V for his rebellious acts and all his estates were forfeited to the crown. With yet another death sentence hanging over him, he did what he did best and made his escape south. Initially he fled to the safety of the heavily guarded Tantallon, where Margaret was presumably already living, and while other members of the Douglas clan fled into exile; he stood firm. The king was furious that Angus had managed to make his escape so he dispatched heralds across the country to proclaim Angus's treachery and confirm there was a reward for anyone who could return his 'base-sister' to their mother. Whether this came from her maternal need to have her daughter close or whether James wanted her in Scotland and away from the English court we cannot know. The legitimacy of Margaret had already been settled by the Pope, so for the king to continue to use the term 'base-sister' was callous and suggests they never shared a close relationship – in fact, it is not too far of a stretch to assume they never even met. It is almost certain they did not meet during their childhoods, with Margaret in one household with her mother and the king in another with the regent, who would have moved between palaces and castles; their paths may simply never have crossed.

Despite this, and out of loyalty to his mother, the king sent 8,000 men to besiege Tantallon and bring Angus and Margaret back to

Stirling. Unfortunately, when the forces arrived, they discovered the fugitives had already departed. Accounts from this time tell us Angus left before his daughter, but before he did he left her strict instructions on how to make her escape with Isobel. Knowing there were soldiers combing the land in search of her, and using Tantallons strategic location on the cliff edge, he ordered Margaret to wait until dusk before making her way down the steep cliff path to the shore where a small boat would be waiting to take them to safety further down the east coast. This must have been a daring and frightening escape for Margret as she found her way in the dark on an uneven path, knowing once false step could have seen her plummeting into the sea below or alerting someone of their escape. Margaret must have trusted her father to keep her safe, there is no evidence to suggest she disobeyed his rules or ever tried to make her escape back to her mother, despite having the opportunity to do so. Over the next few months Angus led the king's troops on a merry dance through the border regions while evading capture.

Regardless over concerns of her legitimacy, Margaret was hot property when it came to marriage and despite only being 13 years old her mother was trying once again to marry her off to one of her allies. She was hoping for a union with her new brother-in-law James Stewart and must have hoped that by making the betrothal, Margaret would be returned to her but Angus was never going to agree to this, or any other suggestion she might have come up with. Apart from anything else, they would have to find Margaret first and as the king's men had shown, that was no easy task. What can we take from her mother's suggestion of this marriage? It does seem a strange proposition to make, mother and daughter marrying brothers is a bizarre suggestion and he came from such lowly stock she was perhaps underselling her daughter somewhat. By the laws of the day the marriage of Margaret was not for her mother to bestow, that privilege lay with Angus as her father.

The fugitives spent much time roaming across the borders, avoiding soldiers where they could. These were desperate times and Margaret found herself sleeping where she could, at times this included barns and outhouses – a far cry from the luxury in which her English cousins were living. The net was starting to close in and Angus became desperate to get his daughter to safety. Realising how valuable she was and the threat she was under, he decided to send her to England and to the protection of her uncle Henry. Henry and Angus had already formed a good relationship so he would have felt comfortable entering England knowing Henry would not decline his request for help.

Angus's first decision was to send Margaret on to the safety of Norham Castle with Isobel. Norham Castle was an English stronghold, it sat high up on rocky ground overlooking the river Tweed and thankfully Roger Lascelles, the steward of the Earl of Northumberland, was happy to take Margaret into his safe keeping. Norham had been besieged by the Scots in 1513 when much damage had been done – it was described by Lascelles as having not one room that did not leak rain in from the roof. Despite its poor state of repair, Margaret entered Norham Castle sometime before 9 October 1528 and stayed there for eight months in the best level of comfort Lascelles could muster for her. During this time, Angus was holding out against the king's forces at Tantallon trying to negotiate a safe return; in December 1528 a treaty was reached between King James and his uncle King Henry, in which it was agreed that James would take all the Douglas lands in return for a pardon for Angus. Sticking to his side of the bargain, Angus surrendered his beloved Tantallon to James, but the promised pardon was not forthcoming so Angus fled back over the border into England. He arrived back at Norham Castle and immediately took Margaret to Berwick.

All of sudden, now back on English soil, Margaret was treated with deference and respect. She was third in line to the throne after Princess Mary and her mother, so her importance and safety were paramount. Angus was aware that he had not yet secured his daughter's future at the English court so, after ensuring Margaret was settled at Berwick Castle in the protection of Sir Thomas Strangeways, he travelled south to London with his brother George. Strangeways was in charge of Cardinal Wolsey's household at Berwick and so agreed to take care of Margaret, knowing he was her godfather. Angus implored him to keep Margaret safe and to not allow her too many freedoms lest she be kidnapped by Scottish border raiders working on behalf of her mother or the king, her brother. Just as when her mother had fled to the borders years before, Lady Margaret now faced the threat of kidnap by the Scots. On the face of it, it looked like she was being kept prisoner but this level of security was a necessity to keep her safe. She may not have been as important in Scotland, but in England she was royalty and despite not holding the title of princess she was treated as though she was. Once again Margaret's life altered just by the crossing of a border, this time, however, she would not cross this border again for a very long time.

There was much sympathy for Lady Margaret Douglas in England; she was seen as an innocent child who had had to flee her home to a country of which she had scant memories, leaving behind her mother and everything she had known. There was no doubting that at this age Margaret was a Scot, she had grown up speaking the language and adopting Scottish customs, but she was going to have to learn to become English. She would have been told by her mother that her Uncle Henry would be her protector, and this was true; both Henry and Wolsey were concerned for her safety and vowed to help her, which would have brought her some reassurance as she sat at Berwick awaiting further news from her father.

Much to Angus's relief he was well received by Henry who offered to pay him and George an annual salary of £1,000 to aid in their roles as spies. Henry wanted to undermine the Scottish government and he now had the perfect agents to employ in this task. In return, Henry told Angus he was on his side against his sister in the matter of their divorce which he felt was morally wrong and much to Angus's delight, Henry wasted no time in summoning his niece to London where he made every effort to accommodate her. Henry's agreement must have brought much comfort to Angus, he knew Margaret needed stability and comfort and he could happily leave her at the English court knowing that she was safe from the influence of her mother and brother. He may not have been heavily involved in her early life, but he had done right by his daughter by bringing her to Henry and could return to Scotland with a clear conscience. Strangeways, who had not received any monetary compensation for Margaret's upkeep while she had been with him, escorted her to the capital, arriving on 6 April 1530. In Henry's eyes Margaret was to be brought up in the style according to her station and part of this meant looking the part of a princess. He ordered gowns from the royal wardrobe and arranged for new ones to be made in opulent fabrics and colours, French hoods, hose, shoes and numerous ribbons, thread and cloth. He also agreed to pay all the expenses of her household including the wages of servants and all the trappings as befitted her rank. Lady Margaret Douglas had arrived at the Tudor court.

Chapter 5

Tudor Cousins Reunited

Margaret's arrival in England came at a time when things were tense at court, the 'Kings Great Matter' was the topic of discussion, he was battling the church in his bid to divorce his wife, who by that time kept to her rooms while Anne Boleyn and her supporters held court. Margaret was not to stay at court; first, she was sent to live with her aunt Mary, Duchess of Suffolk. The duchess was openly opposed to her brother's actions against the queen and did not attend court very often, preferring to stay at her country estate Westhorpe Park in Suffolk with her children, while her husband (and the king's closest friend) Charles Brandon, Duke of Suffolk, did attend. At her Aunt Mary's home Margaret finally had family to engage with; the Suffolk's had three children, Frances, Eleanor and Henry, the Earl of Lincoln. Margaret would have enjoyed spending time with her cousins along with Princess Mary, who was also a regular visitor.

Those three tiny babies who first met nearly fifteen years before in the royal nursery were finally reunited as they stood on the threshold of adulthood. It was in these early happy, carefree days that Lady Margaret and Princess Mary forged a friendship that would last a lifetime. They would have related to each other's plight and no doubt Margaret was somewhat of a curiosity, speaking the way she did. There were many similarities that connected the two young ladies, they were close in age with just five months between them with Margaret being the elder. But they also understood what it was like to grow up with parents with marital issues, albeit in different circumstances. Princess Mary was devoted to her mother Katherine of Aragon, and was distressed by her father's actions, becoming inconsolable when Henry had her removed from her mother's care. With Margaret having been somewhat forcibly removed from her mother by her father, she could relate to Mary's situation more than anyone else. Both were also devout Catholics and would remain so for their whole lives, despite it being dangerous to do so.

Regardless of the ongoing tumult of the king's divorce from Katherine, or the 'King's Matter' as it had become known, it must have been a glorious time for the Tudor cousins, all together once more under the same roof with the diversion of play and education offering a timely distraction for Margaret and Mary, who were trying to adapt to a whole new way of living. There was never any hint of animosity between the elder cousins, they obviously provided a crutch for one another as they gingerly forged a new path for themselves in an ever-changing world. Mary had been the sole object of her father's devotion, he may have longed for a son and wished to be rid of her mother, but there is never any suggestion that Henry was anything other than a loving father. That love and affection was now to be borne out on Margaret too, with Mary more than likely grateful to have someone her own age she could trust and confide in. At some point in 1530 Margaret was sent to live in Princess Mary's household, either at Hunsdon or Beulieu, becoming her chief lady in waiting. Henry ensured she was correctly attired for her new role and provided her with sumptuous new gowns that any princess would be honoured to wear.

It had been decided the two royal ladies were to be taught together by Margaret Pole, Countess of Salisbury. Margaret Pole was cousin to their grandmother, Elizabeth of York, and as an older lady would have been well-respected and revered by Henry. As the daughter of George, Duke of Clarence, and niece to Edward IV and Richard III, she had royal blood in her veins and as the last member of the House of Plantagenet she would prove to be a good role model for them both. She was in her late fifties by the time they came into her care and she was probably traditional in her approach to their upbringing and education.

When Margaret arrived at the English court the contrasts between her and Princess Mary were stark; despite being so near in blood, their lives up to this point had been vastly different. Margaret had spent months living in cold draughty castles on the borders with no luxuries and her accent would probably have been one of the first things to change, it is thought Margaret spoke with a thick Scottish accent making it difficult for her new acquaintances to understand her. Margaret would have been encouraged to speak in French while she mastered a better English tongue, although it is thought she never truly lost her Scottish accent. The princess and Margaret would have spent much of their time at Beaulieu and Hunsdon and would only have visited court for special occasions such as Easter and Christmas. They would have enjoyed hunting together with hawks, playing cards, probably for money, and dancing.

Margaret would prove to be a tower of strength for Princess Mary during her parents' separation, but cleverly did not get drawn into any public debates surrounding the controversial breakdown of the king's marriage, and by doing so kept in his good graces. Wolsey failed in his attempts to secure Henry his divorce and a warrant was issued for his arrest; he died before Henry could send him to the executioner's block. Margaret's thoughts on her godfather's fall from grace and death are not recorded, but he had shown her much kindness and she may have wept privately for him. Instead, the marriage between King Henry and Queen Katherine was finally annulled on 23 May 1532 by Archbishop Thomas Cranmer, and as a consequence of this the Princess Mary was declared illegitimate and removed from the line of succession. This act inadvertently moved Margaret to second in line after her mother and so she took precedence over her cousin. How long she would remain in that position would depend on the birth of the baby Anne Boleyn was carrying at the time of her marriage to Henry; that baby was a girl named Elizabeth.

In the June of 1532 Mary, Duchess of Suffolk, passed away; she had been a much-loved aunt of Margaret and Mary, but without her guidance the two young ladies found themselves in very different positions. The Lady Mary, as she was now to be known, saw her household disbanded in the December following her outright refusal to acknowledge Queen Anne as her mother's successor, or Princess Elizabeth's place as heir. Her father was adamant she should be punished for her disobedience and would deal his eldest daughter a cruel blow when she was sent to wait on the infant Princess Elizabeth.

For Margaret, she had to cultivate her own path at court; on the one hand she would not have wanted to be disloyal to her friend, but at the same time understood that if she wanted to remain in favour she had to conform to the will of the king. Her position afforded her the role of first lady of honour to Queen Anne and Chief Lady of the Bedchamber to Princess Elizabeth – in fact, she would hold this role for all of Henry's subsequent wives. She would also have been expected to swear allegiance to the Acts of Succession and Supremacy which in effect acknowledged Elizabeth as the only legitimate heir to the throne. The Lady Mary refused point blank to do this, as had Sir Thomas More and he paid the price with his head; his execution broke Henry's heart but refusal to take the oath was illegal and punishable by death. That raised a very sensitive question, would Henry put his own daughter to death for her refusal? Blood meant much to the king and even though his daughter's refusal caused him much hurt he would never contemplate carrying out punishment to the full letter of the law. Thankfully, the Lady Mary did not hold this against Margaret despite it meaning the two were forced to part ways.

The good-natured relationship Margaret enjoyed with Queen Anne would have been appreciated by Henry because the queen was not popular and her court was tense and full of intrigue. Anne's status would have been further cemented by having a person of Margaret's standing in her household for she was respected and well liked. Unfortunately, joining Queen Anne's household would prove to be the first of Margaret's numerous downfalls; her behaviour had been exemplary since she joined her uncle's court during which time she had sidestepped potentially tricky situations and never became embroiled in any scandal that could have brought her to ruin – that was until she met Sir Thomas Howard, uncle to Queen Anne. Margaret was going to have to hope the king's good graces stretched beyond just his daughter, because she was about to fall headlong into a disgraceful disaster that threatened to ruin her.

Chapter 6

A Scandalous Love Affair – Part One

Sir Thomas Howard was a younger son of the 2nd Duke of Norfolk and his second wife Agnes Tilney. He was just over three years older than Margaret and it is supposed they met at the christening of Princess Elizabeth in 1533, where he was given the honour of bearing the canopy over the royal infant. Over the next few years, encouraged by Anne Boleyn, Margaret and Thomas would play the courtly dance of flirtation but it would take until 1535 before the relationship between them developed in to more than just flirting. We can follow how deeply they fell in love through the pages of a book of poetry.

The Devonshire Manuscript was a book that contained love poems written by the ladies at the court of Queen Anne. It consists of 124 pages on which 184 poems had been lovingly written out and it is thought that at least two of them had been composed and written by Margaret and six by Thomas. The other contributors were Queen Anne's cousin, Mary Shelton, and Mary Howard, Duchess of Richmond and daughter-in-law to King Henry. Between them they copied out poems, rewrote many famous poems, including ones by Geoffrey Chaucer, and composed their own. In total, it is thought sixteen were written in Margaret's own hand. Sir Thomas Howard was a competent poet himself and it is almost certain the two bonded over their shared love of poetry. The manuscript offers us an exciting glimpse into courtly love at the time of Anne Boleyn, it shows us how the love affair between Margaret and Thomas blossomed and how it quickly developed into something that ended in dramatic circumstances.

The pair were playing a risky game by allowing themselves to fall in love, being the niece of the king and a potential heir to the throne meant that Margaret was not free to fall in love as and when she pleased. She was an important pawn to be played in the political marriage market and any husband she took could one day sit beside her on the throne of England, but the lovers chose to ignore this and continued their affair in secret. It is difficult to say for certain what Henry's initial thoughts on Margaret and Thomas's romance were, it would appear that he knew of the affair and seemed to give it his blessing, but perhaps he did not understand just how far the affair had gone because in a later letter he vents his fury at his niece. He might also have been indulging Anne, but as her power started to fade, so did Henry's acceptance of this dalliance.

Thomas Howard was the younger son of a duke and, with little wealth, had no future role in politics or at court; with his niece Anne's marriage to Henry declining fast, it is unlikely that Henry would have wanted to marry Margaret to a member of the power-hungry Howards, though for them it would have been a powerful match. Regardless of the king's thoughts the two lovers continued to see each other in secret, which would indicate the king had no idea what was actually going on. They even went as far as entering a pre-contract in a ceremony that was witnessed by others, making it as legally valid as any marriage ceremony. The couple also exchanged love tokens, she gave him a miniature portrait of herself and a diamond, while he gifted her a cramp ring – a ring that was worn to ward off sickness. There is no evidence to suggest they ever consummated their union, despite having entered into the pre-contract which would have allowed them to do so without scrutiny. However, it would appear they were waiting for the marriage to be blessed by God before doing so, and this would turn out to be Margaret's saving grace, for if they had, Margaret's reputation would have been damaged beyond repair. But in reality, the damage was already done. Many thought that Howard was using Margaret to further his own desires for the throne, backed by his powerful family and with Elizabeth declared illegitimate following the breakdown of her parent's marriage, Margaret all of a sudden became a very important person in the line of succession.

During the time of Margaret and Thomas's courtship the reign of Queen Anne fell, with disastrous consequences. Anne had failed to provide the king with his much-desired male heir and when the queen miscarried a male child on 29 January 1536, Henry was furious; he looked upon the failure as God's way of condemning his second marriage. Henry had fallen out of love with Anne and set his sights on one of her ladies in waiting, the rather meek and mild Jane Seymour. The problem for Henry was that he needed a way out of his marriage with the queen, a marriage he had traded the religion of the country for, and in order to achieve this he turned to his secretary, and enemy of Anne, Thomas Cromwell.

An annulment would not go far enough and the argument for a divorce based on religion was a non-starter considering the near disastrous events following the divorce from Queen Katherine. So, the king needed Cromwell to arrange a divorce for him using the fact that Anne had been pre-contracted to Henry Percy before she married the king. Much to Cromwell's delight, other rumours had started to circulate around the court that the queen had been having liaisons with men other than her husband. These revelations left Cromwell with no choice, he had to act. It was even suggested that the queen had been involved in a sexual relationship with her brother George, Viscount Rochford, and before long other names were being added to the list. The accused were Francis Weston, a gentleman of the privy chamber, Henry Norris and William Brereton, both the King's Grooms, and Mark Smeaton – a musician the queen was known to like. Anne was known to be flirtatious with men and Cromwell used this as leverage against her, he slowly and quietly began to collate his evidence against the queen, building a dossier of information he could present to the king.

Whether Margaret was interviewed as part of this investigation we do not know; her status may have protected her from this and Cromwell was known to respect her so may have chosen to omit her from his enquiry. It is likely he bribed many of those he interviewed or twisted their stories to meet his needs. While Cromwell was working behind the scenes to bring Anne down, everything seemed to be normal, she had no inclination of what was happening and the king gave no outward sign that he was unhappy with his wife. That was until 1 May 1536, when the king and queen were in attendance at a jousting competition.

At some point during the day Henry was handed a message, he promptly rose and left without a word to anyone; we can only assume this came from Cromwell with confirmation of the news Henry had been anticipating. The arrests were soon made, including Anne's, and the accused were sent to the Tower of London to await trial. The queen stood accused of adultery, incest and perversion which she resolutely denied. The jury, which included her own uncle, found her guilty of high treason and she was sentenced to death along with her brother, Norris, Weston, Smeaton and Brereton. The king did show some mercy towards his wife and requested a master swordsman be brought from France to carry out her beheading. After agonising delays, on 19 May Anne was led from her lodgings at the Tower of London to her place of execution; she remained dignified until the end. There is little evidence to support Cromwell's findings and it is well known he used torture as a mechanism to extract false confessions; he saw an opportunity to bring the queen down and, in the process, bring down his enemies. With the fall of Queen Anne complete, Margaret all of a sudden became a person of extreme importance and seeing how swiftly the king had dealt with his wife it would have worried her greatly.

On 4 July 1536 the Act of Succession was passed which formally declared the marriage between Henry and Anne invalid and as a result Princess Elizabeth's fate went the same way as her elder half-sister Lady Mary. This new act allowed the king to name his own heir, and with his three surviving children declared bastards (his son Henry, Duke of Richmond had been born to Henry's mistress Elizabeth Blount in 1519, he died in July 1536 aged 17), Margaret suddenly found herself a step from the throne. She had gone from being an inconsequential half-sister of the king of Scotland to the threshold of the English crown.

On 30 May 1536 the king remarried and Margaret became the first lady in the court of the new queen, Jane Seymour. At some point after mid-June, however, the king discovered the secret of the pre-contract and was livid; Margaret was now his heir which meant any liaison with the wrong person could be dangerous. Henry was angry that Thomas Howard had thought himself important enough to marry Margaret, the king's niece, and the fact that he was a relative of Anne Boleyn's would not have helped. Margaret did not escape Henry's wrath either, he was angry and disappointed that she had gone ahead without consulting him and both were to feel the full force of his fury. Prior to this, the crime of arranging a royal marriage was not illegal. A royal did not need to seek the monarch's approval in advance but this event unnerved Henry and made him realise what could happen if they did marry. Therefore, he had it written into law that a member of the royal family could not marry without prior approval from the monarch and it became a treasonable offence if the law was broken, making this the first Act of Attainder to legislate on royal marriages. A royal marriage was often made for the benefit of the realm and the gift was considered to be the monarch's privilege; every royal marriage since has required permission of the monarch.

The Act of Attainder was brought by parliament against Sir Thomas Howard on 8 July 1536, the charge being 'making a privy contract of matrimony between the Lady Margaret Douglas and him'. He was arrested for treason and taken to the Tower of London. Henry perceived Thomas's plan was to marry Margaret in order to gain wealth and power for himself and his family and to see himself on the throne next to Margaret, but it is clearly evident from the poems that Thomas loved her, so the idea he did this solely for power is a little far-fetched. When Thomas was interviewed by Sir Thomas Wriothesley, he confirmed that he and Margaret had been in love for the past year, and that they had exchanged love tokens. Just hours later Margaret also found herself a prisoner in the Tower although her arrest was done very quietly; it was kept so low key that it took quite a while for her absence at court to be noticed. As a lady of high rank, she was lodged in relative comfort and would have been allowed a certain level of privilege, such as having her lady's maid with her, but as she looked out over the bloodstained Tower Green thoughts of Anne Boleyn's execution just weeks earlier must have terrified her. She knew her uncle to be a ruthless man who would not hesitate in carrying out the rightful sentence.

Sir Thomas Howard was found guilty of treason, at which time the Act of Attainder was passed, the words are a scathing attack on Howard stating:

> Lord Thomas falsely, craftily and traitorously both imagined and compassed that, in case our sovereign lord should die without heirs of his body, which God defend, the said Lord Thomas, by reason of marriage in so high a blood, and to one such witch pretendeth to be the lawful daughter to the Queen of Scots, should aspire by her to the dignity of the imperial crown of this realm.

As a result of the Attainder, he was placed under sentence of death as was the law, but as Margaret was implicated in the same crime she was also sentenced to death. In the eyes of the law – and of Henry – she was just as guilty as Thomas. This new rule made the treatment of Margaret and Thomas appear extremely harsh. Reginald Pole, cousin to Henry and son to the Countess of Salisbury, publicly pointed out that the couple had not technically broken any law at the time of the pre-contract, and so had been condemned under a statute that was not in force at the time of their offence. Any execution, therefore, would be deemed very unwise.

During Margaret's incarceration in the Tower, Cromwell had been ordered by Henry to remind her that it was he who was paying for her upkeep. Even as a prisoner, she was Henry's responsibility and there were concerns she was keeping too many servants. On the 12 August, Margaret wrote in response to Cromwell addressing these concerns:

> My Lord,
> What cause have I to give you thanks, and how much bound am I unto you, that by your means hath gotten me, as I trust, the King's Grace his favour again; and, besides that, that it pleaseth you to write and to give me knowledge wherein I might have his Grace's displeasure again, which I pray our Lord sooner to send me death than that and I assure you, my Lord, I will never do that willingly that should offend his Grace. And, my Lord, whereas it is informed you that I do charge the house with a greater number than is convenient, which I assure you I have but two more than I had in the court.

Margaret may have entered the Tower of London as a strong-willed young woman but it is clear from this letter that she had learnt a very valuable lesson. In order to facilitate her release, she had to renounce all her loving feelings towards Thomas and she wrote further on this matter to Cromwell:

> And I beseech you not to think that any fancy doth remain in me touching him, but that all my study and care is how to please the King's Grace and to continue in his favour. And my Lord, where it is your pleasure that I shall keep but a few servants here with me, I trust ye will think that I can no fewer than I have, I have but a gentleman and a groom that keeps my apparel and another than keeps my chamber and a chaplain that was with me always in the court.

It is clear that Margaret was desperate not to antagonise Henry any further. This letter also provides us with a first-hand look at how a lady of her station was treated as a prisoner. She was certainly not hard done by and goes on to explain who else she has in her company, keen to point out that she does not keep the company of men and to reiterate she is still a virgin:

> And, my Lord, as for resort, I promise you I have none except it be gentlewomen that comes to see me, nor ever had since I came hither; for if any resort of men come, it should neither have become me to have seen them, nor yet to have kept them company, being a maid as I am.

Upon hearing of her daughter's imprisonment, Queen Margaret wrote to her brother pleading with him to treat her fairly, reminding him that she is of his blood and if he is that displeased with her, he can send her back to Scotland – that was one thing Henry would never agree to. Part of her letter reads:

> Dearest Brother,
> We are informed lately that our daughter, Margaret Douglas, should by your Grace's advice, promise to marry Lord Thomas Howard, and that your Grace is displeased that she should promise or desire such thing and that your Grace is resolved to punish my said daughter and your near cousin to extreme rigour which we can no way believe considering she is out natural daughter, your niece and sister unto the king our dearest son who will not believe that you will do such extremity upon your own, ours and his being so tender to us all three as our natural daughter is.

It is a struggle to think King James would have pleaded that hard for his sister. It is well known the two were never close, but their mother would have been extremely concerned to think her daughter could suffer the same fate as Anne Boleyn. There are no records remaining to tell us how Angus reacted to his daughter's brush with the law, no doubt he would have appealed to Henry to be lenient and reminded him that he had entrusted Margaret into his care. The last thing he would have expected was for Henry to harm her in any way, regardless of the crime committed.

In the end Henry decided against carrying out the punishment to the full extent of the law, his exact reasons are not recorded but it's likely he realised that carrying out the sentence on the two young lovers would have been very unpopular. It was not the fact that Margaret and Thomas had fallen in love that angered Henry so much, it was the fact they had arranged their marriage in secret, making it look as though the couple had something to hide, which in hindsight they did. Also, Margaret was now a valuable commodity to Henry; she was a useful bargaining chip should he have needed one. Despite reneging on the death sentence Henry continued to keep Margaret and Thomas locked up in the Tower at his pleasure; they were still to be punished but as the union had gone unconsummated and with no proof that they were part of a wider conspiracy, he was happy to leave them languishing as prisoners. It would also appear that this scandal left no lasting damage on Margaret's reputation, men still wished to court her and it seems this was never an issue during the discussions of her eventual marriage, she was too great a prize to let a young love affair dissuade any man from marrying her. This whole episode illustrates just how important Margaret was to Henry, to her mother and to England.

This period was a turbulent time for King Henry; not only had he executed his wife and imprisoned his beloved niece, but he also had to come to terms with the death of his treasured son Henry Fitzroy (Fitzroy meaning 'son of a king', albeit illegitimate). Henry's illegitimate son was born in June 1519, his mother was Elizabeth Blount, a lady-in-waiting to Queen Katherine, who at the time of the birth was herself pregnant; that child would be stillborn. Mystery surrounds the birth of young Henry, he was born in Blackmore, Essex, and it would appear not much was to have been made of his birth in terms of celebration but the king openly acknowledged him and Wolsey stood as godfather at his christening.

The birth of Henry was of huge significance for his father for at last he had a healthy son and proved to him that Katherine was the person at fault when it came to providing a legitimate heir. It appears that the young Henry was treated well by his father, in fact he was raised in such a princely manner that you would have been forgiven for forgetting he was illegitimate. His father lavished gifts on him, including his own London residence where a household was set up for him. In 1525 the king went a step further and created his son the Duke of Richmond and Somerset, conferring these titles on him was a clear sign that Henry was happy to acknowledge him – but would he go as far as naming him his heir? At the age of 14 Fitzroy married Mary Howard, the only daughter of the Duke of Norfolk, that marriage was never consummated.

As time went on and no legitimate son was born to Henry many started to look towards Fitzroy as a possible candidate for the role of King. Sadly, just as the Act to disinherit Princess Elizabeth was going through parliament, Fitzroy died. That Act gave Henry the power to name his own heir, although there is no evidence to suggest he would have named Fitzroy, just like he never actually named Margaret his heir. Fitzroy died of consumption (tuberculosis) on 23 July 1536 at St James's Palace, he was buried without ceremony at Framlingham Church, Suffolk. Fitzroy had been living proof that Henry could sire a strong healthy boy and his death would have devastated his father. With him gone and Mary and Elizabeth both disinherited, Margaret once again moved a step closer to the throne – making her dalliance with Thomas Howard even more scandalous.

Relief for Henry came with the birth of Prince Edward in October 1537. This was a relief for Margaret too as it meant he finally had his longed-for male heir and she was no longer the heir presumptive and therefore, less important to the crown. There are questions over the exact date she was released from the Tower of London, but it would make sense for her to be released around this time as Henry would have felt his line was now secure; there is also a letter from her mother written to Henry at the end of October in which she says she is glad for her release. However, there are arguments to support a release as early as November 1536 when the Abbess of Syon Abbey writes to Henry agreeing to take care of Margaret, presumably in response to an earlier letter from the king, but this could be seen as prior agreement ready for her release. Either way we can be sure that Margaret was at Syon by November 1537.

After serving a year of imprisonment in the Tower, Margaret's health was in decline and Henry moved her upriver to Syon Abbey, which sat on the northern bank of the Thames, to convalesce. She was taken into the care of Abbess Agnes Jordan where she could recuperate and regain her strength, not necessarily as a prisoner but more as a patient, Henry was now back to being a concerned uncle and even footed the bill for her medical expenses of approximately £35.00 to Dr Cromer. Shortly after her release Margaret learnt that Thomas had died in the Tower on 31 October 1537, and even though she had earlier renounced all her feelings for him in the letter to Cromwell, she was devastated. Henry granted permission for his body to be taken by his mother from the Tower on the understanding that he be buried without grand ceremony; he was laid to rest at Thetford Abbey in Norfolk. Margaret appeared to bear no grudge against her uncle for imprisoning her for over a year, she hoped to regain his affection through good behaviour; Henry told his sister that if Margaret mended her ways; he would be good to her. He stuck to his word and invited her back to court where she resumed her role as one of the court's most senior ladies after the queen. Once again, she dressed in fine clothes and come new year was grouped with the king's other children in the gift roll. He clearly doted on Margaret and probably felt let down by her behaviour, but there was an obvious affection between the two and Margaret knew if she wanted to remain in his good favour, she was going to have to behave herself.

The whole affair with Thomas Howard showed Margaret to be a headstrong young woman, which probably endeared her to King Henry, but also one who was liable to recklessness, one who was willing to take untold risks. She courted danger and intrigue and probably felt she was invincible; she knew her uncle loved her dearly and more than likely assumed he would always deal with her kindly, many described Margaret as being courageous, others would call it recklessness. She must have known the risk she was taking in entering a pre-contract with Thomas, she was an intelligent woman and it is difficult to think she would have acted without calculating the risks beforehand. These attributes, coupled with the fact that she was part Tudor, part Douglas, part English, part Scottish meant she held ambitions that spanned two realms, she was also well aware of her worth and value and what that worth could accomplish in the future.

But the marriage of Margaret was a huge political issue and there were many names bandied around court of prospective suitors. Cosimo de Medici, Duke of Florence, was one such name but at this time Henry's preferred husband for his niece was Don Luis of Portugal; following discussions however, neither proposal was accepted and Margaret remained unwed.

The king was also unmarried following the death of Queen Jane, the court had been plunged into deep mourning and her passing had a profound impact on Henry. He began to comfort eat and gain weight, this marks the start of Henry's physical decline and presents us with the image we associate with him today. The extra weight gain led to increased pain in his leg, he suffered greatly with ulcers that developed from old sporting injuries that never fully healed, they often wept with pus and could create an awful smell. The pain and anxiety he suffered also caused him to have violent mood swings. But the king could not remain unmarried for too long, he may have his son but in order to really feel secure he needed a second and so decided to remarry, looking to the continent for his new bride. With no queen at court Margaret found herself with no one to serve and she more than likely left court, perhaps she went to stay with Lady Mary.

Henry took time to decide on who his next wife would be, deciding which alliance would benefit England the most would be the deciding factor. In the end he decided to make his fourth wife, Anne of Cleves.

Anne was the second daughter of John III Duke of Cleves, but it was her brother William that Henry was keen on aligning himself with. He was considered a leader of the Protestant cause in western Germany which could help protect England from attacks from the Catholic forces of France and the Holy Roman Empire. Cromwell was keen for this alliance too and pressed Anne's case with Henry and soon preparations were underway to bring Anne to England.

Along with twenty-nine other high-ranking ladies, Margaret rode out to meet Anne at Deptford, following delays due to bad weather in Calais she finally left France on 27 December arriving at Rochester on New Year's Day 1540. Impatient to meet his new bride, Henry rode out to Rochester to meet her and present her with gifts, sending Sir Anthony Browne ahead of him to let Anne know the king was on his way. Upon his meeting with her Sir Anthony clearly foresaw a problem; it is claimed 'he was never more dismayed in all his life to see the lady so far unlike that which was reported'. He decided to keep quiet and not forewarn the king that all was not well, hoping Henry would overlook the fact that his new queen in no way resembled her 'likeness' in the miniature painted by Holbein. Unfortunately, Henry did not hide his disappointment, he left Rochester after speaking no more than twenty words to Anne, instead he returned to Greenwich the next day leaving the gifts with Sir Anthony to pass on. The king confessed his disappointment to Sir Anthony stating: 'I see nothing in this woman as men report of her, and I marvel those wise men would make such a report of her as they have done.' On 3 January Margaret left Greenwich Palace along with a host of other dignitaries to officially welcome the new queen to London. She led the procession down to the foot of Shooters Hill where tents had been erected for the occasion, accompanied by the Earl of Rutland and the Duchesses of Suffolk and Richmond. She was presented to the new queen as one of the premier ladies of the land, she was appointed as chief lady of Queen Anne's household.

It was not to be a position she would hold for long as the marriage lasted only a short while, Henry separated from Anne and the marriage was annulled in July 1540, just six months after the wedding ceremony. Anne went from queen to the 'king's sister' and Cromwell lost his head for his role in bringing her to England. Henry was not to remain unmarried for long, on 28 July 1540 he married the teenage niece of the Duke of Norfolk, Catherine Howard. Once again Margaret found herself being appointed chief lady of the queen's household, a role she shared on this occasion with Agnes Tilney, Queen Catherine's step-grandmother and mother to Thomas Howard. Catherine's ill-fated marriage with the king would not only bring her own downfall but would also embroil Margaret in yet another disastrous love affair.

Chapter 7

A Scandalous Love Affair – Part Two

Margaret was part of the royal progress of 1541 which was scheduled to travel north as far as York where a proposed meeting between King Henry and his nephew, King James V of Scotland, was due to take place. For one reason or another, this meeting never happened. How Margaret felt about potentially coming face to face with her half-brother we cannot know, but as they had never shared a close relationship it is hard to imagine she felt excitement at the prospect. Their mother, Queen Margaret, on the other hand was pleased James would finally come face to face with his uncle and was vocal in her support of the meeting which was scheduled for September. Henry waited patiently at York for weeks for the arrival of his Scottish counterpart and no doubt got angrier as time went on. James pulled out at the last-minute claiming he was worried for his safety in England and even went as far as accusing Henry of plotting to kidnap him, this infuriated Henry even more and put an end to any plans of the two kings ever meeting. Queen Margaret was at a loss to understand how things had got to this stage and became concerned Henry would retaliate with force.

Queen Margaret had enjoyed a relatively calm period once her son had claimed the throne in his own right, she settled into married life with Methven and saw her estates fully restored to her. Sadly, this was not going to last when in 1537 history repeated itself and she discovered that her husband had a mistress. Lady Janet Stewart was the sister of the Earl of Atholl and the mother of Methven's illegitimate son and, just like Angus before him, Methven saw fit to install his second family in one of Margaret's own residences where he siphoned money from her to his own coffers. Money once again became a bone of contention for Margaret, she complained of Methven and of her son, who she accused of leaving her short of funds while he was in France. As she had all those years before, she turned to her brother for support, but he wanted to know the truth of what was happening in Scotland so he sent Ralph Sadler north with a gift of £200 and a mission to delve deeper into the affairs of his sister.

No doubt she regaled him with accounts of how hard done by she had been and that she had once again been forced to endure poverty thanks to yet another unfaithful husband. Once again she contemplated divorce but James was not interested in listening to his mother's rants against Methven, he was trying to come to terms with the loss of his new bride Madeleine, who had died just six months after their wedding. History continued to repeat itself; when the king refused to grant his mother's wish for a divorce she flounced off in the direction of the border, claiming she would leave Scotland forever – although it's hard to believe she actually meant this, she would not have walked away from her son again considering how hard she fought for him. This time the king's forces caught up with her and returned her to Stirling to face her son's wrath. The loss of James's support hurt Margaret, but he managed to persuade her to drop all talk of a divorce. Margaret and Methven never lived together as man and wife again but at least for the time being all talk of divorce was over. Henry continued to ask for updates on his sister's wellbeing, but from Margaret's perspective she was hard done by – she felt her son and brother had both deserted her and sided with Methven. For them, the blame for the situation Margaret found herself in lay solely with Margaret herself; they felt she had let her heart rule her head and had made some questionable decisions as a result.

It was during this great progress that Margaret Douglas learned of her mother's death. Margaret Tudor, dowager queen of Scotland, died on 18 October 1541 at Methven Castle, aged 51. Her cause of death has been attributed to a palsy (stroke) four days earlier. It is reported that her son, who was at Falkland Palace, desperately tried to make it to Methven Castle but sadly arrived shortly after she died.

We have no firm evidence to indicate what kind of relationship mother and daughter shared but Margaret did try to intercede with Henry on her daughter's behalf during the Thomas Howard scandal, and they were more than likely in regular correspondence with one another. But as they had not seen each other in thirteen years it seems unlikely they would have shared a close relationship; it must have brought Margaret some comfort, however, to know she was in her mother's thoughts at the end of her life. Despite having not seen her for so long, the dowager queen was keen for her son, the king, to look favourably on his half-sister; she requested those present in the death chamber to 'solicit from the king, her son, from her, to be good unto the Lady Margaret Douglas, her daughter, and that she might have of her goods, thinking it most convenient for her, forasmuch as she never had no thing of her before'. It was her express wish that she received her jewels as stipulated on her death bed; sadly, James did not heed his dying mother's wishes and passed the jewels to his wife, Marie de Guise. He had no desire to make contact with his sister and certainly did not want anything of value going into Douglas – or English – hands. Margaret did, however, receive her mother's illuminated Book of Hours given to her by her father King Henry VII thirty-eight years earlier. James arranged his mother's funeral, it was a regal and stately occasion as befitted her rank as a queen of Scotland and princess of England. The loss of a parent is always difficult and Margaret would have mourned her mother greatly; it was one more link to Scotland that had been severed.

Once the court arrived back at Hampton Court in November, Margaret found herself at the centre of another scandal which coincided with the downfall of another queen. She had formed an attachment to Charles Howard, brother of the queen and nephew to her first love Thomas Howard. The affair more than likely started at some point during the royal progress and, not deterred by her past experiences, Margaret went head first into another scandal that could have ruined her, with no chance of redemption from the king. Due to Henry's devotion to Catherine, Charles was riding high at court but everything was to come crashing down as rumours of the queen's infidelity began to spread. Catherine stood accused of improper conduct with Francis Dereham prior to her marriage to Henry, and having committed adultery after her nuptials to the king with popular courtier Thomas Culpeper.

On 11 November 1541 Charles was banished from court with no reason being given, but which was more than likely to do with the disgrace of his sister rather than any liaisons with Margaret. Sensing the danger he fled to Flanders, leaving Margaret to deal with Henry's wrath alone. It appears, on the face of it, that this was nothing more than a harmless flirtation, and certainly nothing on the same scale as her love affair with Thomas – Charles himself even stated it was not serious. That's as may be, but Henry was not pleased with his niece's indiscretions; he ordered Archbishop Cranmer to give Margaret a stern talking to, he was to express to her how 'she hath demeaned herself towards the King's Majesty, first with Lord Thomas, and secondly with Charles Howard; in which part ye shall, by discretion, charge her with overmuch lightness, and finally give her advice to beware the third time'. The thinly veiled threat was to be taken seriously; Henry took a lenient approach this time, reprimanding his niece with mere banishment, but he would not be as understanding again. Rather than commit her to the Tower of London, he sent her to the Duke of Norfolk's residence, Kenninghall, in Norfolk, where she was accompanied by her friend Mary Howard, the widowed Duchess of Richmond. The Lady Mary was not permitted to accompany her friend, instead she was sent to live in the household of her brother, Prince Edward. The household of Queen Catherine was being disbanded and Lady Mary took many of her ladies with her, Margaret took none. She was ordered to live quietly and take time to consider her actions; it may have been just a flirtation, but she was in no position to flirt with anyone.

Following investigations Queen Catherine was found guilty of the charges against her and was executed at the Tower of London on 13 February 1542. It was the queen's fall from grace that saved

Margaret from more severe punishment; Catherine's infidelity devastated Henry and he would not have relished having his niece in the Tower as prisoner for a second time when he was going through much personal turmoil. It is worrying to think what punishment he may have meted out to Margaret had he not been under such immense pressure to deal with his errant wife, it appears that once again, Margaret got lucky and managed to escape his wrath. She had ridden her luck twice now and must have heeded the warnings because she stayed at Kenninghall for many months, returning to court in the summer of 1543 at which time the king was preparing to marry Catherine Parr, his sixth wife and final queen. It is easy to look upon Margaret's long absence from court as punishment but in reality, without a queen to serve, there would be no need for her, or any other lady to be residing at court.

Margaret's return to favour was confirmed when she became the trainbearer at the marriage ceremony on 12 July 1543 at Hampton Court. She also became Queen Catherine chief lady-in-waiting, forging a strong friendship with her. The Lady Mary also enjoyed a close relationship with the new queen and the three women will have spent many happy hours together, Margaret was once again, back among a happy close-knit group of like-minded women with whom she could feel comfortable.

Despite two earlier dalliances, at 27, by the customs of the day Margaret was considered old to be unmarried. Having that decision taken away from her she had to wait until Henry felt a suitable match had been found. Once back in favour however, she did not have to wait long. Henry was soon making plans for her to finally marry and her suitor would hail from north of the border in Scotland. He was rumoured to be tall, handsome and a natural soldier. The marriage would of course benefit Henry and England, but it would turn out to be a true love match, much to the delight of everyone.

Chapter 8

Trouble with Scotland

Relations with the Scots had been fragile for some time, in 1542 they defeated the English in the latest round of border raids. Up to this point, Margaret's father Angus had been loyal in his agreement with Henry and had been fighting for England's cause; however, he was soon seeking reconciliation with King James and offered him the privilege of arranging Margaret's marriage for his own advantage. James had always referred to his half-sister as 'base' referring back to her questionable legitimacy to which Margaret took offence causing her to decline any marriage offer he made. She owed her uncle the honour of arranging her marriage.

Border skirmishes were nothing new, but tensions were running high between the two countries and they came to a violent head on 24 November 1542 when the English routed the Scots at the battle of Solway Moss. Despite having higher numbers, the Scottish misjudged the situation and when the English cavalry saw hesitation in their ranks, they seized the opportunity to attack. The Scots found themselves trapped on the banks of the river Esk with nowhere to go, many drowned and around 1,200 were taken prisoner. King James was humiliated by the defeat; his army had been badly advised and soundly defeated, and he had to watch on as they quickly surrendered. In shame, he made his escape to Falkland Palace where he died from a fever on 14 December aged just 30, leaving his 6-day-old daughter Mary as queen. On hearing the news he had a daughter he was reported as saying on his death bed: 'It cam wi a lass, it'll gang wi a lass', clearly lamenting his lack of male heir. The Stewart (Stuart) dynasty did finally end with a woman, but that woman would be Queen Anne in 1714.

Margaret did not openly grieve for her half-brother; she had no feelings towards him other than resentment. She had been badly mistreated by him; he had disinherited her through the confiscation of her father's estates and denied her their mother's jewels, which she had been promised. This was a sibling relationship full of bitterness and hatred, with James punishing his younger sister for the failures of her father. Scotland was in turmoil once again; there was another infant monarch on the throne who would require a regency and with this King Henry saw an opportunity to unite England and Scotland and break the Auld Alliance with France by marrying his son Prince Edward to the young queen under the Treaty of Greenwich. The treaty was in fact made up of two different parts, the first was a list of items that would ensure a lasting peace between the two countries, each would remain independent of the other and retain its own government. The second treaty was to bring about the marriage of Prince Edward and the young Queen Mary. It was agreed that she would remain in Scotland until she was of an age to marry, possibly as young as 10, at which point she would move to England and be brought up at the English court in preparation to become its queen. Delegations from both sides met at Greenwich and signed the document on 1 July 1543, it was later ratified on 25 August 1543. The Earl of Arran, James Hamilton, had signed the treaty on behalf of Scotland, but on 11 December 1543 it was repudiated by the Scottish government. The Scots rejection of the treaty angered Henry so much that he turned to brute force and for the next eight years England and Scotland were at war, this became known as the 'Rough Wooing'. He sent troops north to try and enforce the Treaty, they burned much of the land up to Edinburgh, but this only pushed the Scots closer towards their auld allies the French.

Following James's death, the Earl of Arran was once again appointed regent of Scotland. He decided to recall Angus to Scotland, meaning he was to return home in peace for the first time in nearly thirteen years. King Henry was happy to agree to this as he felt Angus could help broker the marriage in England's favour. It was important from England's perspective that they had the right allies in Scotland because not all Scottish nobles were pro-France; some sought an allegiance with the English believing that peace with a neighbour over the border would be more beneficial as it could bring calmer relations and prosperity. But Henry continued to face resistance to his plans, the marriage proposal was not popular and he needed a new line of attack; finally, the time had come for Margaret to step up and do her duty, her political importance was about to come to the fore. Henry needed a new pro-English faction in Scotland to help push his plans forward so he turned to Matthew Stewart, 4th Earl of Lennox. He viewed him as his new ally and as a husband for his niece. He would have seen Lennox as a safe bet, he would pose no direct threat to his crown but at the same time was a useful man to have in Scotland. There are suggestions that Henry had been in negotiations for some time regarding Margaret's marriage, but how much she knew of the plans, or indeed who her groom was to be, is unknown.

Matthew Stewart was born on 21 September 1516 at Dumbarton Castle, he was a descendent of King James II which meant he had a claim to the Scottish throne through a female line. His father, James Stewart, 3rd Earl of Lennox, had been murdered at the hands of the Hamilton clan at the Battle of Linlithgow Bridge which marked the start of a lifelong bloody feud. Matthew was just 9 years old at the time of his father's death and it was considered too dangerous for him to remain in Scotland so he was sent, along with his brother Robert, to France where they lived under the protection of King Francois I. While in France, they stayed with their uncle Robert Stewart, 5th Lord of Aubigny, he ensured his nephews were well educated, spoke fluent French and enrolled them in the Garde Ecossaise (Scots Guard) where they received military training. Matthew stayed there for ten years, but following the death of James V and the advancement of Arran as the regent, it became necessary for him to return home to Scotland to oppose the rule of the regent. At this stage Matthew was very much pro-French and anti-English and was against any arrangement that might link England and Scotland together.

Regent Arran was now the head of the Hamilton clan and was the half-brother of James Hamilton, the man who killed Matthew's father. He and Matthew both had legitimate claims to be Mary, Queen of Scots' heir, and given her tender age some Scottish nobles asked Lennox to return as opposition to Arran's rule. Many questioned Arran's legitimacy but they knew any opposition to his rule could cause further unrest so warned Lennox to be cautious. King Francois sent Lennox to Scotland as his ambassador, a role that would not raise suspicion, but one in which he would be expected to protect French interests against the English; he finally returned home in April 1543.

Lennox soon realised there was very little support for him or his cause in Scotland and in a bid to gain some power he offered his hand in marriage to the widowed Marie de Guise, mother to the queen. His proposal was met with a firm rebuttal as he was deemed far too inferior for her, after all she had been queen and would be looking for a husband of a much more elevated rank than an earl, an issue that had not bothered her mother-in-law. It would not have gone down well with the nobles either, Arran would never have sanctioned such a match on his enemy, it would have given him too much power and leverage to overthrow his regency. Marie de Guise saw the sense of not remarrying, her priority was her young daughter and if she stood any chance of becoming regent for her, she would have to remain unmarried.

Lennox was frustrated, he felt thwarted at every turn and soon started to look towards England for support – and his attention soon fell on Margaret. He approached Angus, seeking approval to offer his hand in marriage to his daughter but as a potential heir to the English throne, and despite being the heir to the Douglas clan, she was a member of the English royal family and so it was King Henry's permission he needed to seek – it would also be Henry who provided the marriage dowry on behalf of his niece. In order to make his intentions clear Lennox approached the English ambassador Sir Ralph Sadler in the hope he would push his suit with Henry. Luckily for Lennox, Sadler considered him a worthy match for Margaret and coupled with the fact he was willing to make an alliance with Angus, he urged Henry to give the proposal some serious consideration, which he did. He saw how beneficial this match could be in strengthening the ties between the two countries and in bolstering the chances of the marriage between Prince Edward and Queen Mary.

Unfortunately, Lennox was not the kind of man to tie his allegiance to one side if the other still made lucrative offers to lure him back to their fold. Marie de Guise gave him fresh hope that marriage was back on the cards, it suited her at that time to have him fight her corner and with a force of 10,000 men, he confronted Arran at Linlithgow. He managed to secure the safety of Marie de Guise and the young queen and escorted them to Stirling Castle where, on 9 September 1543, Mary was crowned in a hastily arranged coronation in the Chapel Royal conducted by Cardinal David Beaton, Archbishop of St Andrews. Lennox was given the honour of carrying the sceptre at the ceremony. If the marriage was to go ahead, the queen would become his stepdaughter and potentially provide him with untold power; any marriage to Margaret would be well and truly usurped, as would any alliance with England. But it didn't take long for Lennox to realise there was going to be no marriage and that he had been used yet again by the Scots; he turned his coat once again back to Angus, the English and Margaret. The constant changes in allegiance worried the English who were now extremely wary of Lennox and the ease with which he could change sides. The issue of trust was one of concern for Henry, he had to be certain that Lennox was a man of honour, not just in terms of his allegiance to the country but to Margaret too. The English council were worried if he had turned his coat once, he could quite easily do it again.

Lennox wanted Henry to help him regain his title and estates in Scotland but knew he was going to have to prove his worth. He made the bold claim that he would march on Edinburgh and confront Arran again; he had successfully done it at Linlithgow so it could be done again, except this time he would have to face the French too. King Francois had pledged his support to Scotland by sailing six ships full of ammunition and money up the Clyde to assist Marie de Guise in her fight to gain control. Any loyalty Lennox had left for the Scottish or French was gone when he was removed from the governor's council. He got his revenge by intercepting the French ships and making off with the money and most of the weapons on board. This was the clearest sign yet to England that Lennox was fully pledged to their side, he would continue to work for Henry but in return he wanted assurances from the king that he would be sufficiently compensated for his losses in France and Scotland. He was willing to help the English capture Dumbarton Castle on the west coast, and Dunbar Castle over on the east. Both were impregnable fortresses in strategic locations and helped in controlling traffic in and out of Glasgow and Edinburgh respectively and whoever held them held significant power. But as far as Lennox was concerned until those reassurances came, he would continue to hedge his bets and communicate with both sides.

Relations between England and France were at an all-time low and Henry made plans to invade Boulogne in the summer of 1544. In the February of that year, he gave his assent to a new Act of Succession which restored the Lady Mary and Lady Elizabeth to the line of succession, but crucially it made no mention of the heirs of his elder sister Margaret Tudor and her Scottish descendants. The Act allowed Henry to alter the succession in his will, which he wrote shortly before he set sail. He stated in his will that should Edward, Mary and Elizabeth produce no lawful heir, then the line of succession would be settled on the heirs of his younger sister Mary Tudor. He had cut Margaret and her heirs out of the succession completely; however, it must be noted that at no point did Henry ever include Margaret in the line of succession or name her as his heir, these were assumptions only. The fact that she descended from the Scottish line was not the only reason Henry may have wanted to bar Margaret from the throne; at this stage he did not trust Lennox, he saw him as a turncoat and simply could not trust him with the throne of England, he may not have wanted it for himself but if his wife sat on it then he would look to rule through her.

There was no great fall from grace and the rumours of a rift between Margaret and her uncle also seem to be unfounded. Thomas Bishop, Lennox's secretary, later seems to have alluded to the fact that the pair had fallen out but Bishop was no fan of Margaret's and the pair were constantly at odds with each other. She accused him of being a troublemaker and once she was married, he thought her too influential over her husband, constantly undermining his hold over Lennox. There was definitely no love lost between the pair and despite being dismissed from the Lennox household at some point after 1546 he would be a thorn in Margaret's side for many years.

The English still harboured hopes that there would be a marriage between Prince Edward and Queen Mary but it was clear the Scots were never going to agree to this, instead they turned to France and the infant son of the dauphin Henri. The new Act of 1544 underlined the fact that if Queen Mary wanted to sit upon the throne of England, then she was going to have to marry Prince Edward.

Chapter 9

Marriage to Matthew Stewart, 4th Earl of Lennox

The Tudors were not a successful family when it came to making a good marriage. Other than King Henry VII and his wife Elizabeth of York there seems to be an everlasting battle to be happy. Young Prince Arthur died just weeks after his marriage to Katherine of Aragon which would later be used against her as her second husband Henry VIII attempted to divorce her. Henry's struggles with marriage are well known but his elder sister Margaret fared no better when her first husband King James died in battle and her next two, Angus and Methven, were both unfaithful to her. Their younger sister Mary Tudor did her duty to the family and her country by marrying the aged king of France, she had been in love with Charles Brandon but Henry had forbidden them to marry. When the king of France died, Mary and Charles married without Henry's permission, his punishment was an exorbitant fine and banishment from court. King Edward VI was too young to marry, but his elder sister Queen Mary did. Unfortunately, her husband could not wait to leave England once it became apparent she was not going to provide him with an heir. Queen Elizabeth seems to have learnt from her family's mistakes and decided to remain unmarried. But for Margaret things were to be different; hers was an arranged marriage but it was a successful and happy one too.

After nearly a year of negotiations, the terms of Margaret's marriage to Lennox were finally agreed upon. Lennox and his supporters were to spread the word of God throughout Scotland, in other words they were to ensure the Catholic faith was enforced.

Henry might have broken with Rome but he saw the Protestant faith as heresy, he wanted to be Head of the Church of Scotland; Lennox was to remain loyal to the king and to England, and they were to renounce all previous loyalties to France and Scotland; Queen Mary was to remain in Scotland until a time when she was to be delivered to Henry to marry Prince Edward; to assist England in capturing strategic border towns and strongholds; to help Henry become protector during the queen's minority. In return for this Henry would send an army north to Scotland and make Lennox governor under his protectorship; Lennox would receive vast revenues to help maintain his status and should Mary die without issue, Henry would send help to Lennox to claim the throne. If Lennox could agree to these terms, then Henry would declare himself 'contented' for his marriage with Margaret to go ahead. Rather surprisingly however, he stated that he would 'never cause her to marry with any but whom she shall find in her own heart to love'. In other words, if Margaret did not like the thought of marrying Lennox, then the whole deal was off. This is an astonishing claim to make given how important her marriage was dynastically. It is also further evidence to suggest the pair shared a deep affection with one another. Maybe after two doomed love affairs he felt she deserved to marry for love, but maybe only someone he loved too and in Lennox it would appear the right bridegroom had been found to satisfy all parties, happily, Margaret readily accepted the proposal. For Margaret there was the possibility that one day he could place the Scottish crown on her head, while alternatively she could place the English one on his, the dynastic outcomes were extraordinary.

Much to everyone's delight, Lennox readily agreed to the terms and signed his agreement on 17 May 1744, setting sail from Scotland on 28 May and travelled down the northwest coast of England, arriving in Chester on 7 June. From there he rode to London where he joined up with the court at St James's Palace on 13 June and it was here that he was first introduced to his bride – they hit it off instantly. They made a striking couple, Margaret was considered a court beauty, she was tall and slim and had the signature Tudor flame coloured hair, while Lennox was handsome and charming with blue eyes and auburn hair. He was an accomplished soldier, and no doubt had the physique to match; he was a courtier but was ruthless and ambitious, while she was an illustrious member of the court and many sought her patronage making them a true power couple. Lennox declared his love for Margaret before they had even been introduced, he may have been in love with the idea of marrying a member of the Douglas clan as it brought him back into the Scottish fold somewhat. For Margaret, the match with Lennox reconnected her to her Scottish roots. Lennox signed the marriage treaty on 26 June at Whitehall and they married in the presence of King Henry and Queen Katharine Parr on 29 June 1544 in the chapel Royal at St James's Palace. Following the ceremony there were jousting competitions and celebrations to be enjoyed by the whole court. Lady Mary gave Margaret a selection of religious-themed jewels including a ruby, diamond and pearl pendant, a gold and ruby brooch and a gold and emerald brooch. Margaret would treasure these gifts for the rest of her life. Following the lavish banquets, the couple were publicly put to bed as was custom for the time.

Henry remained true to his agreement to compensate Lennox for his lost estates and granted the newlyweds property in the north of England, the chief estates being Temple Newsam near Leeds and Settrington House which sat about thirty miles from the coast at Scarborough in Yorkshire. Henry was shrewd – giving them substantial lands in the north was no accident, other than providing his beloved niece with rents that would give her a good standard of living, Henry hoped that by placing them there Lennox would be able to halt any potential rebellion like the Pilgrimage of Grace of 1536. The north of England was a Catholic hotbed and they had been known to rise against the monarch in defence of their faith, Henry may have dealt with those rebels of 1536 but the threat of uprising was ever present as the shifting face of England's religion threatened to dominate the country and its people for years to come.

As well as numerous properties, he also lavished them with money and expensive clothing, including cloth of silver. Upon her marriage Margaret was created the Countess of Lennox but was very much treated as a princess, and it seems Henry continued to put her on an equal footing to his daughters in terms of providing for her even after her marriage.

On 10 July 1544 Lennox became an English citizen and Henry wasted no time in returning him Scotland to push his vision of a united throne, he was tasked with taking the castle at Dumbarton as per the terms of his marriage agreement. There had also been news that Angus had abandoned Henry due to the loss of Douglas lands in the border region and had thrown his lot in with Arran, his new son-in-law's biggest enemy. Angus's troops beat the English at the battle of Ancrum Moor in February 1545 which won him favour with the Scottish lords, it also impressed Francis I and he awarded him France's highest chivalric honour, The Order of St Michael. The rift between Angus and Henry put Margaret and Lennox in a difficult position: Angus was her father but Henry had done so much for them, not only was he her uncle but her sovereign too. Naturally, her loyalties lay with Henry and England and therefore so did Lennox's.

An English defeat in Scotland was a rare occurrence and Henry had no option but to retaliate and so turned to Lennox to help. He provided him with sixteen ships and 600 men to go north to restore order. When he departed from Bristol in early August, Lennox may have known Margaret was already pregnant with the couple's first child. Now she was a married woman with her own estates to run, her education was finally paying off, she had a large group of retainers and an army of servants to help her in maintaining her land and gathering her vast rents. Life was good for the new Countess of Lennox, she was in high favour, a newlywed, pregnant and wealthy, she must have felt that at the age of 28 she was settled. But life in Tudor England did not remain settled for long.

The news from Scotland was not good. Unfortunately, Lennox did not succeed in taking Dumbarton for the English, neither did he succeed in revenging his father's death; the Scots soon discovered what he was about, they attainted then exiled him. Despite his failure Henry assigned him the task of going north to Carlisle to enter discussions about the potential marriage between Prince Edward and Queen Mary but again all attempts were in vain, he even failed in his endeavours to bring Angus back into the English fold. In the October of 1545 Lennox was officially attainted by the Scottish parliament for his recent attempts to destabilise the country; he, along with his younger brother Robert, were accused of treason. He saw his lands and title revert back to the crown and his finances took such a hit that he and Margaret would feel the pinch of financial strain for the rest of their married life. Despite having his title officially removed the couple continued to style themselves as the Earl and Countess of Lennox. It had not been a good start for Lennox in his bid to prove loyalty to Henry, anything he tried north of the border seemed to end in failure as he was outwitted by the Scots, who saw him as nothing but Henry's English servant. Regardless of his failures Margaret stood by her husband and remained his most loyal supporter and it is just as well she did, for who knows what the reaction from Henry would have been otherwise; no doubt Margaret protected her husband from the worst of Henry's anger.

In England, things had not been easy for Margaret either. She had been parted from her new husband shortly after their wedding and was pregnant with their first child, she first lodged with Queen Katherine before moving to the royal palace at Stepney as her pregnancy advanced. The pregnancy was not easy, Margaret suffered greatly with various conditions throughout her term for which she received copious remedies from the Royal Apothecary Thomas Alsopp, sadly they did not to help and Margaret went into early labour at about 7–8 months. After a hard labour a baby boy was born in late February 1545 and was given the name Henry and the title Lord Darnley. The little boy had not been strong from birth and died in London on 28 November aged just 9 months old without either parent being with him. Much to Margaret's distress she had been at Temple Newsam preparing for the birth of her second child when he passed away. It could not have been an easy time for her, Lennox spent many months away from his wife and son and following baby Henry's death, Margaret's own health began to decline to the point of her needing regular medication from Alsopp. The two pregnancies and births in quick succession seem to have taken their toll on her.

Chapter 10

Birth and Loss

In preparing for the birth of any of her children it is likely that Margaret followed the customs of the day and entered confinement around four to six weeks prior to the birth. She would have been locked in an inner chamber where all natural light was shut out using thick tapestries and there would be a fire blazing, no matter the weather. No men were allowed in the birthing chamber prior to the birth and only the husband would be permitted afterwards. The process of childbirth was very much the business of women. Margaret would have been attended by a midwife and some of her closest female companions; although no records remain to tell us who these women were, they were usually those who had been through childbirth themselves or female relatives.

The business of childbirth in the Tudor era was perilous and Margaret knew this only too well. First, there was the pressure of the sex of the child, as King Henry could testify. If you were a high-ranking lady, then providing a son and heir for your husband was important in continuing his lineage, and it would have been the mother's fault if she failed in this. There was also a realisation that she would more than likely have to go through it all again until a boy was safely delivered. Whether or not to have a child was not a discussion that would have taken place; a man was expected to marry and the sole role of his wife was to produce a male child.

The role of the mother in a high-ranking Tudor family would have been limited. Straight from birth the baby would have been passed to a wet nurse while the mother regained her strength. It was custom for the baby to be baptised shortly after birth, infant rates of mortality were high in Tudor times, as Margaret well knew, and in order for a baby to enter heaven it was imperative they were baptised as soon as possible. The mother would not attend the baptism, even if the birth had been straightforward, she was required to stay in her chamber until about six weeks after the birth when she would have been churched. Churching was a ceremony of purification and thanksgiving and would been undertaken regardless of the outcome of the birth, the mother could not leave confinement until she had been blessed by a priest. Once she had, she could return to normal life leaving the care and upbringing of her newborn baby to an army of nurses. We can assume Margaret followed this routine as she left 8-month-old baby Henry in London in the care of nurses while she travelled north to Temple Newsam to give birth to her second child. Why she chose to have the child there rather than in London we do not know, but given the weakness of baby Henry and Margaret's struggles, it may have been thought beneficial for her and her baby to take the cleaner country air. It was not unusual for noble parents to spend vast amounts of time away from their offspring, they usually had numerous estates to run and would regularly travel between them leaving their children in the nursery at their principal residence in the country or at their London residence when at court. The education of the boys would have been carefully planned out and great care taken by the parents in choosing the right tutors for the right subjects. For girls, their education – if they were lucky to have one – may have been given by the mother, she would have been much more involved in her daughter's upbringing than her sons.

Despite suffering challenges during her pregnancies Margaret seems to have come through each delivery with few physical difficulties, although the mental toll it must have taken would have been heavy. There are no records detailing the births of any of her children, but we know she gave birth to four girls and four boys; the names of her daughters are not recorded but she lost six of her babies in infancy and must have felt as though God was not on her side.

By December 1546, Margaret was living at her principal residence Temple Newsam, which sits to the east of the city of Leeds in West Yorkshire. Her second son was born there on 7 December 1546, like his older brother, he was named Henry and was styled as Lord Darnley, unlike his elder sibling he was a strong baby who thrived from birth. We don't know much about the birth of Lord Darnley but we do know Henry stood as his godfather and he was to be brought up in the Catholic faith as per his mother's wishes. Margaret was always someone who understood her role in life and she instilled this into her eldest son, she made sure he was fully aware of his royal status and brought him up as any prince would have been. His education would be an important part of his upbringing and from a young age he was given tutors: John Elder taught him Latin and John Lallart taught him French. As Margaret found out when she came to the English court, it was important to be able to converse in more than one language. Darnley's education did not stop at learning classics and languages, it is said that he excelled at sport, which given his athletic frame and lean legs is not surprising. He was an accomplished horseman who enjoyed hunting and hawking, like his mother had in her time at Tantallon. He was trained to joust, engage in swordsmanship and games such as tennis and golf. It is said he also enjoyed music, playing instruments and singing and no doubt he was also an excellent dancer. He had auburn hair and was well known for being handsome with a lean physique. He was also very tall, standing at over 6ft which was extremely rare for the time.

Despite the dynastic hopes of his parents and his exemplary education Darnley was an oaf. He was arrogant, petulant and lazy to name just a few of his negative traits. He was also a liability; he had no common sense and was often found to be telling those around him the plans that were being made regarding his future. He was known to have a violent temper which was apparent when he did not get his way; if thwarted, he would become childish and immature. He was openly homosexual and conducted many affairs after his marriage to Queen Mary, including when she was pregnant with their child. He is described by some as being 'mentally and morally weak'.

For all his weaknesses Margaret and Lennox either failed to see the shortcomings in their son or chose not to acknowledge them. To his parents he was the golden child who held their dynastic hopes in his feeble hands. If they had seen what he was like and offered him the guidance he clearly needed, his marriage and future may have been so very different. But the legend of Darnley has created an almost romantic hero, a troubled soul who was brutally murdered at a young age. The importance of Darnley's birth should not be underestimated, he was English by birth which gave him a legitimate claim to the throne as well as claims to the earldoms of Lennox and Angus north of the border. He was the nearest male Tudor relative to the king after his son which made him a forerunner to succeed Edward should he die without issue. The only problem was that Darnley was being raised a devout Catholic, which meant Edward would not contemplate him taking the throne; he even discounted Princess Mary based on her religion meaning he was ready to defy his father's wishes over the succession. In order to protect her young son from court politics, Margaret kept him safely in the north at Temple Newsam where he was given a princely education as befitted his rank as a member of the English royal family.

Margaret was to suffer more heartbreak when King Henry VIII died on 28 January 1547 at Whitehall Palace in London. His reputation as a tyrannical monarch who sent two of his wives to the block is well established, but to Margaret he had been a constant source of support and protection from a young age and despite incurring his displeasure on a couple of occasions, he treated her as well as any princess could have wished for. He lavished gifts on her, took care of her household expenditure and ensured she was brought up fully aware of her birth right. They had enjoyed a close relationship; it is said that Henry saw many Tudor traits in her: her flame red hair, her tall stature and her ability to be headstrong and decisive were all characteristics he admired. Before he died there were rumours circulating that Margaret had fallen out with her uncle; a letter to Cecil from Thomas Bishop, written at a later date, recounted an instance in which Margaret had threatened to remove Bishop from the Lennox household. Bishop then turned to Henry for support and he supposedly sided with Bishop against his own niece. Bishop alludes to the fact that Henry was angry with Angus for his betrayal and he was taking his anger out on Margaret, Henry had treated Angus more than generously and he would not forgive this betrayal easily. Bishop saw himself as one of the king's most loyal subjects, assisting in getting Lennox to come over to the English side for which he was handsomely rewarded by Henry, he gave him a respectable manor house in Pocklington, East Yorkshire, as well as a pension of £60 per year. Bishop also accused Margaret of trying to rule through her husband. If she did behave in this manner then Lennox showed no outward signs of it; their marriage was happy and always appeared to be on an equal footing, Lennox respected his wife's influence at court. Whether this supposed fall out was true or not we do not know, was Bishop trying to score points over Margaret? Quite possibly, we know there was no love lost between the pair so it is not too far a stretch to think he would stoop so low as to try and upset the relationship between Henry and Margaret. Also, given Henry had forgiven Margaret her indiscretions in the past, would he really want to punish her for the deeds of her father, a father she had not supported when it came to the crunch? Bishop felt bitter he had been usurped and he wanted his revenge; in his mind, Margaret was responsible for his removal and he felt undermined by her, but she was a strong-willed woman who was stubborn in the face of attack – she was not to be trifled with.

When Henry died Margaret mourned him deeply, he was a father figure and a constant fixture in her adult life and after his death she continued to speak kindly and affectionately about him. She was also keen to remind her father how he had been good to their family in their hour of need all those years before. She hung his portrait alongside one of Princess Mary at Temple Newsam. But for now, there was a new monarch on the throne, King Edward VI inherited the throne at the age of just 9 years old and Margaret was soon to find that her role at court was going to be very different under his rule.

Margaret, like her close friend Lady Mary, was a devout Catholic and having a base in the north of England made her a figurehead for those who refused to lean towards Protestantism. Temple Newsam had become a safe haven for any Catholic needing to seek refuge from the zealous rule of King Edward and the Lord Protector, the Duke of Somerset, but it seems that as long as they did not openly question the king's rules or ideas pertaining to religion, they were left alone. It was her religion that kept Margaret away from court for much of Edward's six-year reign, she had not developed a close relationship with him and when she visited court to present the young Lord Darnley to the king, he received her coolly. As a known Catholic at a court with no queen, she found herself unwelcome and unneeded so, she retreated back to the safety of Yorkshire and her estates. For Lennox, he never really associated or aligned himself with any religion in the same way his wife did, he was born a Catholic and later converted to Protestantism but never practised in either religion which meant when Somerset came knocking on his door to help with Scottish affairs, he was more than happy to help and remained in favour.

Somerset was keen to reignite the war with Scotland and was eager for his nephew King Edward to marry Queen Mary, and so he enlisted Lennox, in a bid to lead a two-pronged attack. Lennox was based at Carlisle and was to go forth to attack the west coast while the Protector would lead the attack from the east. On 10 September 1547 the forces of England and Scotland met on the banks of the River Esk near Musselburgh at the battle of Pinkie Cleugh. Somerset, along with the Earl of Warwick, had 18,000 men at his back who marched from Berwick to Edinburgh, and warships hugging the coast. The Earl of Arran met him with nearly 22,000 men blocking the route to Edinburgh, the two sides faced each other in what was to become the last pitched battle between the two countries. The English cavalry attacked first and were bravely fought off by the Scots, but before long the English artillery started to batter the Scottish army back which soon began to collapse. They lost nearly 6,000 men, compared to

Margaret Tudor, Daniel Mytens, c. 1620–38, Royal Collection Trust © *Her Majesty Queen Elizabeth II, 2022*

Archibald Douglas, 6th Earl of Angus, unknown artist, c. 1500–99, Royal Collection Trust © *Her Majesty Queen Elizabeth II, 2022*

Margaret Douglas, Countess of Lennox, unknown artist c. 1572, Royal Collection Trust © *Her Majesty Queen Elizabeth II, 2022*

Matthew Stewart, 4th Earl of Lennox. *Public Domain via Wikimedia Commons*

THES BE THE SONES OF THE RIGHT HONERABLES FERLLE OF LENOXE AD
TE LADY MARGARETZ GRACE COVNTYES OF LENOXE AD ANGWYSE,

1563

CHARLLES STEWARDE
HIS BROTHER, ÆTATIS, 6,

HENRY STEWARDE LORD DAR-
LEY AND DOWGLAS, ÆTATIS, 17

Henry Stewart, Lord Darnley and his brother Charles Stewart, Earl of Lennox, Hans
Eworth, 1563, Royal Collection Trust © *Her Majesty Queen Elizabeth II, 2022*

Mary Queen of Scots. *Public Domain via Wikimedia Commons*

James VI & I (1566–1625) c. 1620, Paul Van Somer, Royal Collection Trust © *Her Majesty Queen Elizabeth II, 2022*

Above: The Memorial of Lord Darnley, Livinius de Vogelarre, 1567, Royal Collection Trust © *Her Majesty Queen Elizabeth II, 2022*

Below left: The Darnley Jewel or Lennox Jewel c. 1571–8, Royal Collection Trust © *Her Majesty Queen Elizabeth II, 2022*

Below right: Arbella Stuart as a child, artist unknown. *Public Domain via Wikimedia Commons*

Above: Linlithgow Palace Detail, 2022 © *Christopher Adams*

Below: Linlithgow Palace, 2022 © *Christopher Adams*

King Henry VIII, after Hans Holbein the Younger, c. 1537. *Public Domain via Wikimedia Commons*

Mary I, Henry Shaw, c. 1840–70, Royal Collection Trust © *Her Majesty Queen Elizabeth II, 2022*

Elizabeth I as a Princess c.1546, Attributed to William Scrots, Royal Collection Trust © *Her Majesty Queen Elizabeth II, 2022*

Catherine of Aragon by Wenceslaus Hollar, 1652, Royal Collection Trust © *Her Majesty Queen Elizabeth II, 2022*

Anne Boleyn. *Public Domain via Wikimedia Commons*

Jane Seymour by Hans Holbein. *Public Domain*

Anne of Cleves by Hans Holbein the Younger, c.1539. *Public Domain via Wikimedia Commons*

Catherine Howard
by Hans Holbein
the Younger, 1540.
*Public Domain via
Wikimedia Commons*

Katherine Parr,
Unknown Artist, late
sixteenth century.
© *National Portrait
Gallery, London*

500 losses on the English side. This would be the last battle in the 'Rough Wooing', the Scots signed a treaty with the French known as the Treaty of Haddington in which they agreed that Queen Mary would marry the Dauphin. Ironically, the French ships that bought the soldiers to fight for Scotland were the same ships that later took their young Queen to France. They managed to smuggle her passed the English to Dumbarton and from there she sailed to France where she was to be brought up alongside the Dauphin, they would eventually marry in 1558. By making this marriage she would eventually become the queen of France and Scotland. In exchange, the French promised to offer military support to help drive the English out of Scotland.

With a foothold in the southwest of the country, it was down to Lennox to try again to bring the west under English rule. After a brief reunion with Margaret at Wressle Castle, he again made plans to attack the west coast from his base in Carlisle, where he had left hostages as his insurance against any potential treachery, they were the sons of local border lords. The new plan included a pact with Angus's brother-in-law, Robert, Master of Maxwell. The plan was for Lennox and his men to march to, and take, the town of Annan in Dumfriesshire, which they did. In return Maxwell was to bring with him nearly 2,000 men to meet with Lennox's forces but when Lennox arrived at Dumfries there was no sign of Robert, or his men; it quickly became clear he had reneged on his promise and no help was coming. With no option but to retreat back over the border to England, Lennox left Scotland and returned to Carlisle Castle. When he arrived back, he arranged for four of the hostages to be hanged as punishment; these executions would haunt Lennox's for the rest of his life causing bouts of depression, he never could come to terms with the guilt of ordering the deaths of boys not much older than his own sons. Lennox took no further part in the conflict, faced with yet another military failure he returned to Temple Newsam, to Margaret and their children.

Angus had become disillusioned with Arran and once again turned his attentions to the English; he wrote to Margaret in the June of 1548 informing her the war was continuing. The Maxwells had turned on the English and Angus had beaten their forces at Drumlanrig – but also that Dalkeith had been destroyed, this held significance for Margaret as it was where her mother had first met King James IV. Angus managed to escape back to Tantallon, he warned Margaret that Scotland was a very dangerous place and urged her to remain safe in England.

Following the very public desertion of Lennox and his cause in Dumfries the relationship between Margaret and her father became even more strained. By this time Angus had remarried, he had wed Margaret Maxwell and they had two sons, the eldest they had named James and he now stood to inherit the Douglas lands, disinheriting Margaret in the process. Lennox did not know how best to deal with Angus so he turned to Somerset for guidance, he advised them to make peace with Angus and bring him back over to the English fold. This made sense to Margaret, for if she harboured any hope of inheriting the Douglas titles and lands she would need to be on good terms with her father. Margaret knew exactly what she was entitled to and was not going to give up the right to be head of the Douglas clan without a fight and no doubt Lennox backed her plan.

Margaret was briefly back at court in November 1551 for the state visit of Marie de Guise, dowager queen of Scotland, she was stopping in London having recently visited her daughter in France. Regardless of religion, Margaret was still considered to be a senior member of the court and she was to meet Marie de Guise at the Bishop's Palace, which lay near to St Paul's Cathedral, along with her cousin Frances Brandon, Duchess of Suffolk; the Lady Mary had refused to attend. From the Bishop's Palace they travelled though London to Whitehall Palace where she was to meet King Edward. From Margaret's point of view this could not have been an easy meeting, Lennox was a traitor in Scotland which meant he could not be presented to the dowager queen; Margaret found herself the wife and daughter of traitors.

Angus continued to make attempts at reconciliation with Margaret, even claiming that she 'is the thing in the world that I love best', but despite advice she was not for forgiving her father – her stubbornness once again proving to be her weakness. That was until the spring of 1552, his young son and heir had died and he now reached out to his only surviving child in the hope of forgiveness. Margaret decided she wanted to travel to Scotland to see her father, unfortunately her request was denied by King Edward on the grounds that neither of them could be trusted not to form some kind of plot against his person. Margaret and her family had been under surveillance and the last thing the English government wanted was for them to travel over the border and be out of reach. A second request to travel was declined in the December of 1552, but by the April of 1553 Margaret was finally granted permission to visit her father, on the understanding that Lennox and her children remained in England. She travelled to Tantallon and was more than likely in residence there on 6 July 1553 when the young King Edward VI died. Finally, it was time for Margaret to come out of the royal wilderness and return to court now that her close friend Mary had become queen of England.

Chapter 11

Back in Favour

It was not an easy transition for Mary due to the attempted coup to steal the crown by Lady Jane Grey and her supporters, but knowing it was her birthright and by the will of her father, she raised troops to fight for her right. Mary finally won her crown on 19 July, just nine days after the claim was made by Lady Jane, who was sent to the Tower of London where she was to remain until her execution on 12 February 1554. Queen Mary was finally crowned at Westminster Abbey on 1 October 1553, it is not known whether Margaret attended the coronation, possibly due to being pregnant or having just given birth, but if she did then no doubt her role would have been of some significance. There was much to celebrate; the joy and relief of Margaret and England's Catholic population was immense for they were now free to openly practice their religion, and with Mary now sitting on the throne the Lennoxes were suddenly in high favour. The the new queen bestowed on Margaret clothes and jewels including a diamond worth £500 as a token of her gratitude and in recognition of their lifelong friendship. The new queen ensured her closest friend was suitably accommodated too, she provided her with lavish apartments at Whitehall Palace and like her father had done before her, she paid for their household expenses, including the installation of a kitchen which was conveniently placed over the apartments of Princess Elizabeth, ensuring she was disturbed day and night by noise and smells – a move she may have regretted later. Mary extended her gratitude to Lennox too as she made him a member of the privy council and Margaret, keeper of the privy purse. She even gave precedence to Francis Brandon over Elizabeth whose nose was being well and truly pushed out.

The discussion of who would succeed Mary started almost immediately; she was thirty-seven and unmarried when she ascended the throne so the chance of her producing an heir was slim. By the terms of Henry VIII's will, the next in line would be her younger half-sister Elizabeth, but their relationship was fraught so Mary decided her only option was to marry in the hope that she could give birth to a male heir. On 25 July 1554 Queen Mary married Philip of Spain at Winchester Cathedral. He was the eldest son of Charles V, Holy Roman Emperor, a Catholic and a foreigner, meaning there was much objection to the marriage, nevertheless Mary forged ahead with her plans. In order to bring his son's status in line with his new bride Charles V created Philip king of Naples and Jerusalem, she was now marrying a king rather than a foreign prince. Margaret was the chief lady of honour and bore the bride's train at the wedding ceremony. She was pregnant at the time and when she gave birth to a son, she named him Philip. Following the wedding Margaret accompanied the newlyweds back to London via Windsor and Richmond before re-entering the capital on 18 September 1554.

The reign of Queen Mary brought security and comfort for Margaret and her family, finally they were able to live openly and freely at court where they were popular and well established. Not since the reign of Henry VIII had Margaret enjoyed a permanent place at court, and now she had a husband at her side to share court life with. She took precedence over her cousins Princess Elizabeth and Francis Brandon and Mary was suggesting Margaret be named her heir. It was not just Margaret that looked to advance under Mary, the time had now come for Darnley to be officially presented to the queen. He sent her an example of his writing and in return she sent him a gold chain; as the eldest son of her best friend, he was going to be spoilt, the queen made him a court favourite and she regularly showered him with lavish gifts, which must have delighted his parents. Queen Mary may not have been able to convince the English parliament to name Margaret as her heir but that did not stop Darnley from gently reminding her that he too was perhaps a worthy suitor for the throne. He often wrote to her pledging his allegiance, offering himself for soldierly duties and telling her how passionate he was to serve. No doubt encouraged by his mother.

Mary's reign was far from settled and she faced stiff opposition from some nobles for her Spanish marriage. There were serious concerns that England would return to Catholicism and become a Spanish territory, leading to them interfering with the politics and running of the country. Mary had appointed many prominent Catholics to roles of power within her government, including forty-three to the Privy Council, these moves angered many and the threat of rebellion was real – in 1554 a coordinated uprising would test Mary's resolve and reign to the limit. The Wyatt Rebellion was led by a group of nobles including the Duke of Suffolk, whose daughter Lady Jane Grey was languishing in the Tower of London, Sir James Croft from Herefordshire, Sir Peter Carew of Devon and Sir Thomas Wyatt, a landowner from Kent. It was their aim to remove Mary from her throne and replace her with Elizabeth. The plan was that each leader was to head an uprising in three regions, the Midlands, Kent and the West Country and they would then all converge on London. The idea of three simultaneous revolts was to cause confusion in the government as they would not know which to put down first, which in turn would lead to one of the groups being successful. The French got involved too as it was in their interests to stop a Spaniard from sitting on the throne of England so they offered to block any Spanish ships in the English Channel that may come to Mary's aid or more importantly, let Philip in. Unfortunately for the rebels, news of the plot reached the ears of the Imperial Ambassador Simon Renard and he related the plot to the Lord Chancellor Bishop Stephen Gardner who moved quickly. He brought Edward Courtenay, Earl of Devon, in for questioning as his name had been specifically mentioned by Renard. Devon admitted there was a planned uprising, which was brought forward because the news had been leaked.

The Duke of Suffolk only managed to raise several hundred men and was refused entry to Coventry, he quickly gave up his plans and was arrested. Meanwhile in Kent, Wyatt managed to raise 4,000 men and the Duke of Norfolk was sent to put down the rebellion there, but he failed to do so and retreated back to London. This worried Mary and her councillors into entering negotiations with the rebels. Wyatt demanded control of the Tower of London and of the queen herself; angered by this bold request Mary rallied the people of London to her cause when she gave an impassioned speech at the Guildhall on 1 February. Wyatt delayed in making his advance to London which gave the government the opportunity to shore up the city's defences. He and his forces arrived in Southwark on 3 February but were unable to cross the River Thames at London Bridge due to it being heavily guarded by Mary's supporters. Not to be deterred Wyatt travelled down river to Kingston hoping to cross there but again the bridge had been damaged and his men were forced to rebuild it. They managed to cross to the north bank of the Thames where they faced little opposition. As the rebels approached Ludgate trouble started and they split up, but many got trapped among the narrow streets and panic set in. Wyatt was captured and instantly sent to the Tower of London with the other leaders. Mary demanded swift action and even though she pardoned many of the rebels a total of ninety were executed, including Wyatt and Suffolk. Lady Jane Grey and her husband Guildford Dudley were also executed, even though they played no active part in the uprising she was seen to be a focal point for any future rebellion, a risk Mary was not willing to take.

It had been suggested Wyatt was tortured in an attempt to implicate Elizabeth in the plot, he refused to confirm this but Mary was not satisfied and arranged for her sister to be brought to London for questioning. Elizabeth was horrified to discover she had been implicated and suffered a mental collapse when she heard she was to be arrested. An account of her arrest mentions the terrifying moment:

> Three cabinet ministers whom she deputed to see the
> arrest executed, rudely entered the chamber at ten o'clock
> at night, and though she was extremely ill, they could

scarcely be induced to let her remain till the following morning. Her enfeebled state permitted her to be moved only by short stages in a journey of such length to London.

On 16 March 1554 Elizabeth was taken to the Tower, she beseeched the guards to allow her the opportunity to speak to the queen directly as she did not trust her councillors, but this was refused. She stayed as a prisoner for nine weeks before being released under house arrest. Eventually Mary agreed to meet her sister at Hampton Court but the meeting was to take place under the cover of darkness. She asked her outright to confess her involvement in the plot but Elizabeth remained steadfast and refused, leaving Mary with little choice but to back down and release her sister although suspicion remained over how much she actually knew.

Up in Scotland things were no less fraught, a rebellion against Arran was raging and Lennox had been told if he returned, he would be restored to his titles and land, a promise that had been made so many times before, but after discussions with Mary and her council the decision was made to send Lennox back north in an attempt to turn Arran against the dowager queen to create more in fighting. The English offered their military support to those Scots who wanted change, and backed by Spanish money this was a formidable challenge. In the end Arran revoked his regency and Marie de Guise took the role on behalf of her daughter. The Lennox lands remained in the hands of the crown.

The biggest act to take place during Mary's reign was the counter reformation, England finally returned to Rome in November 1554 which gave much joy to Catholics up and down the country, including Margaret, she and many others were now free to worship openly. Feast days were reinstated, mass could be heard and all the old relics, paintings and vestments were returned to churches along with decorated alters. All the changes made by Edward VI in 1552 were swept away and the old religion in its purest form was reinstated. A return to the old religious ways was important to Margaret, she took her religion very seriously, managing to sidestep earlier issues regarding her refusal to convert to Protestantism. Religion influenced her life in every way: how she lived it and in the decisions she made. She attended mass every day as did her household staff. All the feast days were observed and she fasted on Fridays, observing the sabbath on Sundays.

For those who had embraced the new religion things were about to get very difficult. The return of Catholicism meant Protestantism was swept side and abolished completely and if you were not willing to recant your ways then a very painful death awaited. Approximately 800 people were executed for their religion during Mary's reign, most notably Hugh Latimer, Bishop of Worcester, Nicholas Ridley, Bishop of London, and Thomas Cranmer, Archbishop of Canterbury, who had also been instrumental in bringing about the divorce of Mary's parents. These three bishops were known as the Oxford Martyrs and were burned at the stake for their beliefs. The widespread punishment earned Mary the moniker of 'Bloody Mary', and that is how history remembers her. Like her father their reputations are their legacy and history has a tendency to overlook the other deeds they did during their reigns.

Sadly, for Mary there was to be no child to inherit the throne after her. In the September of 1554 Mary and her physicians had reason to believe she was with child. She displayed all the usual symptoms including morning sickness and weight gain. The baby was due around the March/April of 1555 and she entered her confinement in preparation for the birth. The news broke on 30 April that Mary had given birth to a healthy boy, there was much rejoicing in London at the news, bonfires were lit and the bells rang out but that joy was to be short lived. When Mary remained closeted in the birthing chamber through May and June, it quickly became apparent she had not given birth, in fact she had not even been pregnant, but she continued to cling to the hope that a baby would come, despite her doctors knowing otherwise. By July Mary's size returned to normal. Simon Renard wrote to Charles V to confirm 'the queen's deliverance is delayed and it is doubted whether she is really with child, although outward signs are good and she asserts that she is indeed pregnant'. Mary's reasoning for the false pregnancy was that it was God's will to withhold a child from her until all Protestants had left her realm, this brought about even more burnings. Many pitied her for her delusional ideas but the pressure Mary was under to produce a male heir was immense, not just for England but for Spain too and it is thought that intense desire to be a mother led to her false pregnancy. In the August she finally accepted there would be no child and she returned to court humiliated. Mary was physically and mentally drained by her experience, she was extremely thin and melancholic, she never uttered a word regarding the pregnancy and neither did the court. Philip left England in the September leaving Mary devastated, she was plunged into a deep depression and he would not return until 1557. No doubt Margaret was on hand to offer comfort to her friend and may even have been in confinement with her, but we are not certain of her whereabouts and she may even have been pregnant herself. Sadly, baby Philip died in infancy but Margaret was to give birth to another son, they named him Charles and thankfully he was to survive childhood and reach adulthood.

The following years were happy and settled for the Lennoxes, their life was comfortable and Darnley was thriving, but news from Scotland was coming that would cause Margaret distress and sadness. On 22 January 1557 Angus died at his stronghold Tantallon Castle, in his will he stipulated that his title and estates should be entailed down the male line, he had openly chosen to disinherit Margaret who was his natural and rightful successor. By the terms of the will the new Earl of Angus was his nephew and Margaret's cousin David Douglas. He died not long after inheriting the title and was followed by his son Archibald Douglas who, given his tender age, was placed under the guardianship of the power-hungry Earl of Morton. Angus left nothing in his will for his eldest child which given his obvious love for his daughter is somewhat of a mystery. Naturally this infuriated Margaret, it left her confused and angry and because as she did not get on well with Morton she must have known she stood little chance of negotiating with him. She openly refused to acknowledge the legitimacy of the will, instead she started styling herself as the Countess of Lennox and Angus, given that Lennox was still considered a traitor in Scotland this was a bold move and ran the risk of angering the Scottish government even further. Queen Mary tried to intervene in the dispute, she sent an envoy up to Scotland to negotiate with the queen dowager on the premise that neither Lennox or Margaret held the titles that were rightly theirs by birth. The response from Scotland was that as Margaret resided in England, and had done for most of her life, and was married to a traitor, a Scottish claimant was preferable.

When Queen Mary died on 17 November 1558 at St James's Palace, Margaret was no closer to being acknowledged as her father's lawful heir and now she had to deal with her profound grief at losing her friend. The queen died childless and the ascension of Elizabeth was seamless, Margaret knew she would need to negotiate Elizabeth's elevation to the throne carefully, despite being cousins they had never been close as Margaret's loyalty had always been with Mary. Mary lay in state in the Privy Chamber at St James's Palace for three weeks. Her ladies stood vigil and observed mass everyday praying for the soul of the departed queen. Margaret was appointed the chief mourner and when the funeral possession left the privy chamber for the Chapel Royal, Margaret followed directly behind the coffin with the Earl of Huntingdon and Viscount Montagu at her side, her train was carried by Lady Katherine Hastings. Behind them came the great noble men and women of England, a requiem mass was said with Margaret kneeling to pray on a black velvet cushion. The walls of the chapel were draped in black and forty-six tall candles had been lit to surround the coffin which was placed on a hearse in the middle of the chapel. The queen's coffin was covered in a cloth of gold pall on top of which her effigy was placed, dressed in her robes of state with her regalia as a crowned monarch. Five black horses pulled the cortege through the streets of London to the great west door of

Westminster Abbey. Inside, the Abbey had been draped in black and was lit by candlelight, the Bishop of Worcester blessed Mary's body and she was carried into the Abbey by twelve men. Her body lay in the cathedral overnight, guarded by 100 poor men all dressed in black. The following day, on 13 December 1558, a further requiem mass was heard and Margaret was followed by the great noblemen who approached Mary's coffin where they bowed to their queen, they then broke their staffs of office and placed them in the tomb as the coffin was interred in the Henry VII Chapel. Margaret mourned her friend deeply, not only had she lost a lifelong companion, cousin and queen, but with the death of Mary went any chance of the Catholic religion remaining in England. Before long she found herself having to retreat inwards when it came to celebrating her religion, she had to go back to worshiping in secret and once again found herself outside of the established church of England and on the fringes of court life.

Queen Elizabeth made her grand state entrance into London on 14 January 1559 and even though Margaret was at the head of thirty-nine high-born ladies she was not given the honour of carrying her train, that privilege went to Margaret Audley, Duchess of Norfolk. The time of high favour was over, it had been all too brief and now Margaret and Lennox found themselves with no place at court and were granted permission to leave London and return to their Yorkshire estates. Elizabeth feared Margaret, as she feared all her female relatives that carried the royal blood, she was a suspicious monarch who was constantly looking out for plot against her, thinking she was going to be usurped at any moment. Margaret and Lennox were advised not to contact the queen directly, instead if they wish to communicate with her, they were to do so via her chief advisor William Cecil. The relationship between the cousins was distinctly cool, Elizabeth had clearly not forgotten earlier slights made against her, but regardless of that, Margaret was still a high-ranking lady and could not be dismissed as easily as banishing her to Yorkshire. Margaret was considered a real threat to Elizabeth's power, she was a Catholic to Elizabeth's Protestantism and as throughout the Tudor era, religion was never too far from politics and Margaret was determined to use her religion to her advantage. But she would learn very quickly that Elizabeth was not her father, nor her sister for that matter, and her rule would be very different. The queen was determined not to afford Margaret or Lennox the freedom and luxury they had so far enjoyed out of fear of what they could do – and it would turn out to be a wise move on the queen's part.

Chapter 12

Plotting for Darnley

Protestantism was sweeping Europe. In Scotland, Marie de Guise saw her daughter's kingdom slowly turning away from Catholicism, the preacher John Knox had incited the people of Perth to rebellion, they defaced the city, including the tomb of Margaret's mother. He was against female rule which enraged Elizabeth, it was Knox's view that any man who obeyed the rule of women was seen as a sinner in the eyes of God. This would not bode well for Queen Mary and he would become a key person in making her reign uncomfortable. In a desperate bid to stem the flow of hatred, Marie de Guise turned to her old suitor Lennox. She invited him to return to the country on the promise she would restore him to his title and lands and with Margaret keen to establish a united Catholic England and Scotland they set about making their northern homes a focal point for Catholics. Settrington sat just thirty miles from the coast which made communication with Europe and its Catholic population much easier. Margaret was living quietly in Yorkshire and this worried Elizabeth, she had long been suspicious of her cousin and felt she was plotting something, so, in 1559, she tasked the Duke of Norfolk, the Lieutenant of the North, to set spies in the Lennox household to report back exactly what they were up to. Combined with the spies already implanted by William Cecil, anything Margaret and Lennox did was not going to go unnoticed.

At this stage the Lennox's had no idea their household had been infiltrated with a network of spies, but in her usual strong-willed manner Margaret was not going to allow Elizabeth to persecute her and her family for being Catholic so she pre-empted any attack and turned to the Spanish ambassador Alvarez de Quadra for help.

She told him how she felt about Elizabeth and that the treatment her family were suffering was unjust; given that they had done nothing that could be deemed dangerous to the queen, Margaret could not understand why they had been banished from court. This could be damaging to Darnley and his advancement, and he had a right to be welcomed at court by Elizabeth, given his proximity to the throne. Fed up with life in England and the ongoing battles in Scotland, the Lennoxes contemplated going into a self-imposed exile to the continent, an idea like this would have put Elizabeth on high alert, maybe she had been right to be suspicious of them after all.

As a Catholic with royal blood Margaret was in a powerful position to advance the suit of her sons. Through his parents, Darnley had a strong claim to both the English and Scottish thrones and at a time when Europe was a bubbling pot of religious discontent, with help from powerhouses like Spain, anything could happen. It is widely thought Margaret held mass at her northern homes despite it being illegal, but she was never punished or sanctioned so we can only assume that she gave an outward appearance of conforming to the new religion. Cecil and Lord Robert Dudley, a favourite of Elizabeth, were aware the Lennox homes were a hotbed of religious activity so kept a close eye on developments, but in reality there was no plotting to take Elizabeth's throne from her – at least not at this stage.

Soon enough Margaret would have a reason to start plotting the advancement of her eldest son, Lord Darnley. King Henry II of France died unexpectedly in 1559 which meant Mary, Queen of Scots, was now also queen of France. Never one to miss an opportunity, Margaret sent the 12-year-old Darnley in secret to France with a letter for Mary offering her congratulations and requesting she reinstate the Lennox title and lands back to her husband. The queen refused but the trip was not a wasted one, she gave Darnley 1,000 marks and an invitation to the coronation at Rheims on 18 September 1559. Rumours were strong that the new king was frail and had never enjoyed robust health; Margaret could not have envisaged he would die so soon after ascending the throne but she did no harm to Darnley's cause by sending him to France to make the queen's acquaintance. Despite Mary already being married, the ultimate goal for Margaret was to eventually wed her to Darnley and unite the thrones of England and Scotland after Elizabeth died. Had Mary been looking for a husband Darnley would not have been a bad choice, he had claims on both thrones and could help her realise her ambition of sitting on the throne of England – but that was for the future; at this first meeting Mary had no reason to think on these kinds of matters.

King Francois II did not reign for long. He passed away on 5 December 1560, leaving Mary a widow at just 18 years old; what she would choose to do next no one could guess, but it soon became clear she could not remain in France. There was no role for her there following the king's death and she was a queen in her own right, so her only option was to return to Scotland and take up the reins of power in her own realm, where her mother had also passed away in 1560. When news of Francis II's death arrived in Yorkshire, Margaret knew she had to act quickly; she dispatched Darnley to Orleans to offer his condolences on behalf of himself and his family. At the age of 14 he failed to make the impression Margaret had hoped, the young widowed queen was not interested in considering him as a potential suitor. Darnley returned home to Settrington having not accomplished his mother's goal, but Margaret knew she would have to play a long game. Mary was only recently widowed, she had a specified period of mourning to observe and would take time before considering her next husband. But crucially, Darnley's name was in the frame, all the Lennox family had to do was keep abreast of the situation and act when the time was right.

They were going to have to apply some patience as Mary took her time to decide her next move; she eventually returned to Scotland but when she did, Darnley was not present to welcome her. Margaret felt the time was not right, Mary would need time to establish herself as queen in a realm she had left at the age of 6. Mary had been their queen in absentia and the religious sands were shifting, the transition from French queen to Scottish queen was going to take time. From the Lennoxes point of view, it was time to start plotting. Darnley was young, good looking and, more importantly, he had English and Scottish royal blood running through his veins; he would be the ideal person to marry Mary and become king of Scotland. Elizabeth was on high alert; she sensed a plan was being made and that plan would be to marry the pair of them together and threaten her rule. In order to remind Margaret who held the power she revoked her earlier promise to help Lennox regain his lands and ordered the whole family to remain in England where her network of spies could keep an eye on them, under no circumstances were they to travel to Scotland without her prior permission.

It would appear there was a desire for Lennox to return to Scotland. Thomas Stewart, Laird of Galston, visited the Lennoxes in Yorkshire to advise Matthew they should petition Elizabeth again to help reinstate his titles and land, if that was unsuccessful then they were to petition Mary, where they would find support for Lennox's claim and return to Scotland. Buoyed by this plan Lennox sent Galston to London to push his petition with Elizabeth but she was not interested. This placed Lennox at a crossroads and not knowing what he should do next, he brought Galston back to Yorkshire where Margaret charged him with the task of taking a personal note from the family to Mary in France. He arrived just as she was leaving her official mourning period of forty days, he helpfully reminded her she had an English Catholic cousin of marriageable age should she wish to consider remarrying.

Margaret and Lennox were not stupid, they understood the game they were playing was dangerous and the scrutiny they were under was intense. They even went as far as making a pact with the Spanish which would offer the Lennox family a safe haven should they need to leave the country in a hurry. It would seem Spain was keen for this marriage and de Quadra was happy to push for this alliance on behalf of Margaret and Matthew. It was at this stage that Bishop was dismissed from the Lennox household; angry at being ousted, he offered his services as an informer to the Privy Council who were keen to listen to what he had to say. He was eager to divulge everything he knew, or alleged to know, of his former employers true feelings towards their monarch, he wanted revenge and many of the allegations made at this time come directly from him. He told them Margaret was ungrateful and had no loyalty towards her cousin and that they harboured hopes of a marriage between Darnley and the Scottish queen, putting them on high alert.

Mary finally returned to Scotland, arriving in Leith in August 1561. The country had changed dramatically over the thirteen years she had been away in France, many of the lords were hostile to her rule, given she was a female Catholic monarch in an increasingly Protestant country and she had little knowledge of the volatile nature of its politics. It quickly became evident that Mary could not rule by herself, she simply did not have enough respect from her councillors to reign effectively, she would need to marry to conceive an heir in order to cement her status. The choice of who her husband would be was a topic of conversation across Europe and it seemed everyone had an opinion on the matter. Mary had indicated she was considering a proposal to marry Don Carlos, son and heir of Philip II of Spain, this was a cause for concern for Elizabeth and her advisors as the last thing they wanted was a Spanish threat north of the border. If Mary forged an alliance with a Catholic European power like Spain, the impact on England could be disastrous as they would be sandwiched between that alliance in the north and the French to the south. In a bid to stop the marriage Elizabeth stationed her navy in the Channel and North Sea as Mary sailed from France to Scotland, they wanted to intercept her and bring her to England; they were unsuccessful.

At this stage Darnley was not seen as marriage material for Mary except within the family, there were hopes in Scotland she would marry Arran, though this idea was quickly rebuffed by the council. The mere thought of this infuriated Lennox, making him more determined to marry the queen to his son and Margaret backed this plan wholeheartedly. With Mary now back in Scotland any negotiations for marriage would be much easier and the plotting stepped up a notch. During the early stages of their plotting, Margaret and Lennox continued to court favour with Elizabeth, knowing she would probably be against the marriage they needed to keep her on side in order to keep their plans under wraps. What they did not know was the extent to which Elizabeth's spies had managed to infiltrate their household, all their plans were being reported back to Cecil and the queen. Elizabeth's fears were coming true and she knew she had to act as soon as possible to nip this plot in the bud before it manifested into anything more serious. She arranged for Lennox to be arrested while conducting business in the capital and the rest of the family were summoned to London at once. Margaret initially refused to go but as time went on, she could refuse no longer.

Lennox was initially put under house arrest but was quickly moved to the Tower of London, signalling how seriously Elizabeth was taking this threat. Shortly before his arrest, Lennox decided he no longer wished to portray himself as Protestant and aligned himself instead with the French faction at court, boldly declaring himself Mary's Catholic heir. This further compounded Elizabeth's need to get him and Margaret in captivity as soon as possible, she needed to neutralise their threat and put in place actions to control and monitor exactly what they were doing. Margaret's thoughts must have flashed back to Thomas Howard's incarceration and hoped the same fate would not befall her husband as had befallen him. She was eventually arrested at Settrington in mid-March 1562 and was escorted with her younger daughters and servants to London, Darnley and his younger brother Charles were to be held in York under the supervision of the Duke of Norfolk, although Darnley managed to escape to France where he was protected by fellow Catholics. He more than likely sailed from Bridlington and then on to France, it would have been unwise to join the French court as Elizabeth could arrange for him to be brought back to England, although it is doubtful the French would have assisted her in this. Philip II of Spain was keen to keep Elizabeth onside, he would have been concerned at the Scottish-French alliance and to alienate the English would have been a bad move for Spain. However, the prospect of a Catholic ruler appealed to him, he was going to have to hold his breath and wait to see what happened.

Meanwhile, young Charles was being kept in York under close guard, Norfolk could not risk him disappearing too. Saying goodbye to her sons would have increased Margaret's anxiety, though she had learned to remain calm and recognised the importance of keeping them away from London and out of Elizabeth's reach; she could not, however, carry on defying her monarch's orders. When she finally arrived in London, her servants were sent to the gatehouse prison at Westminster Abbey and Margaret was housed in her apartments at Whitehall Palace. However, when charges of treason and witchcraft were brought, she was removed upriver to the Charterhouse at Sheen Palace where she was to be kept under house arrest under the close guard of the queen's cousin, Sir Richard Sackville. He was a Boleyn relative of the queen's and his loyalty was assured.

Sheen Palace sat on the south bank of the Thames overlooking Syon Abbey. It was established by Henry V in 1413 for use by the Carthusian order of monks but by 1539, following the dissolution of the monasteries, it had passed back to the crown. It was then given to Henry Grey, Duke of Suffolk, and his wife Frances Brandon, and they converted it into a luxury country mansion for their family. When Henry Grey was executed for his role in the Wyatt rebellion, Queen Mary gave the priory back to the Carthusians who stayed there until Elizabeth evicted them, at which point it returned to the crown. Sackville leased a suite of rooms from Elizabeth in 1559 and it was here that Margaret was sent with a small group of servants and her young daughters. De Quadra reassured Margaret that Spain would support them should the situation require an intervention and reiterated their support for any plan to put her or Darnley on the English throne. Philip's soldiers were ready to back this with force, they ardently wished for a return to Catholicism and having Darnley as king would facilitate this seamlessly.

Unfortunately for Margaret, Bishop and some other members of her household had never shown such loyalty to their employers. Bishop drew up a list of fifteen articles that could be laid at Margaret's door which he passed directly to the Privy Council. These articles hinted that Margaret was greedy, ruthless and domineering, and worse still, had her sights set on Elizabeth's throne. He also went on to accuse her of using witchcraft by bringing about the burning of the steeple at St Paul's Cathedral, although this happened after a thunderstorm in which lightning appeared to have struck the steeple. He also pointed out that Margaret should not be seen as a true English subject given that her mother had given birth to her while in flight from Scotland and therefore should not inherit the throne, he also raked up the old illegitimacy issue despite this having been settled years earlier. Not happy with this, he also told of Catholic masses being held at the Yorkshire homes of the Lennoxes where they also encouraged their staff to worship at the Catholic altar. There is no doubt Bishop did a thorough job in divulging all of Margaret's secrets. Rumours were also being circulated that she was preventing Elizabeth and Mary from meeting as she did not want to risk Mary divulging any information regarding the marriage plot to her English counterpart. In order to persuade Mary against it she claimed if she left Edinburgh the English would sweep in and take control. There is no evidence to corroborate this claim and Cecil would never have allowed the two monarchs to meet.

The Privy Council and Cecil took what Bishop had to say very seriously and after eight weeks at Sheen Palace Margaret was questioned over the allegations put to her, she naturally protested her innocence. Cecil's questions were as follows:

1. What communication hath she had of the bastardy of Queen Mary (Tudor) and the queen that is now (Elizabeth) and what words hath she uttered thereon against the queen?
2. When Paul's steeple was burnt, what report was made to her of a certain number of men struck with sudden death in St James's Park?

3. What moved her to say that touching the right to the crown she would give place to none of the rest?
4. What message was brought to her from the Lord Seton concerning his furtherance in setting forth of Lord Darnley?

Margaret did herself no favours when faced with these questions, she is described by Sir Henry Sidney as being 'very obstinate in her answers to the council sent to her'. Lennox was questioned many times while in the Tower but like Margaret he always maintained his innocence. As far as Margaret was concerned, she and Lennox had been very hard done by, they were being held on false charges and ought to be released without any further delay. She continued to petition Cecil of their innocence and also expressed her concerns over the conditions in which Lennox was being held at the Tower. She had been told he was being held in solitary confinement which sometimes led him to be violent towards his gaolers, who often complained of his erratic behaviour. Cecil assured her he got plenty of fresh air and exercise and was being well looked after; as a man of some standing he was more than likely being well cared for, but having been someone who had never experienced capture he more than likely felt claustrophobic.

Lennox was finally released from the Tower and sent to Sheen to be with Margaret and Charles, who by now had been sent from York to be with his mother. They were finally reunited by late November but were still kept under house arrest. Elizabeth, despite suffering from a bout of smallpox was adamant they were to remain at her pleasure. That pleasure was costing them a vast sum of money because as prisoners they were responsible for their own upkeep and had to pay for their lodgings, and food and wages of any servants kept with them; with the estates in Yorkshire being deserted, their source of income had been severely hit. Elizabeth being ill, however, provided Margaret with an opportunity to show concern and loyalty and she offered to leave Sheen to nurse the queen herself.

The evidence against the Lennoxes was overwhelming but Elizabeth was happy to release them both. It is thought Dudley had managed to persuade her to let them return to Yorkshire to live quietly on the condition they would not allow Darnley to marry without her prior consent. Whether Margaret made this oath in the knowledge she would break it, or whether she sincerely expected to adhere to it is unknown but I suspect it is the former. The proposition of Darnley marrying Mary was not forgotten, they may have been shocked by the treatment they had suffered and how close they had come to utter ruin but at the end of the day Elizabeth had freed and forgiven them, which in their eyes left them free to continue to plot. Although we don't know whether, at the time of their release, Elizabeth believed Margaret and Lennox would cease their plotting, it does seem unlikely she would have freed them if she, or Cecil for that matter, had any inkling they were still aiming to go through with their plans. Maybe the persistent nagging from Margaret finally wore Cecil down and it was felt they would be best far away from court.

Elizabeth's illness raised the inevitable questions over the succession and parliament were keen for her to name her successor. According to the terms set out in Henry VIII's will, the crown would pass to the daughters of Frances Brandon, the Duchess of Suffolk. She was the eldest daughter of Mary Tudor and her eldest daughter, Jane, had already been executed for her attempt at gaining the crown, leaving her younger sister Katherine as a valid claimant, but her behaviour had brought her to the Tower of London and her continued defiance of Elizabeth's rules was about to benefit Margaret and her family greatly. Despite holding them prisoners, Elizabeth held back from unleashing the full force of the law on the Lennox family. Her mind was far from made up in terms of the succession and with Katherine Grey in disgrace and Mary being a Scottish Stewart, Margaret, or Darnley, offered a legitimate Tudor heir. Elizabeth wanted to keep her options open and the potential successor in suspense.

Chapter 13

Lennox and Darnley Travel to Scotland

Lady Katherine Grey was the middle daughter of the duke and Duchess of Suffolk, she had already seen her elder sister and father incarcerated in the Tower of London and eventually executed after being found guilty of treason. She had previously been married to Lord Henry Herbert, the eldest son of the Earl of Pembroke, but when Lady Jane was embroiled in a failed coup the earl was keen to distance his son from the Grey family and the marriage was annulled. However, that did not deter the young Katherine from pursuing an illicit lover affair, knowing the potential for further ruin for her family. As a member of the royal family and one of the potential heirs to the throne, as per the law of Henry VIII's legislation on royal marriages she would have needed royal assent to marry. Katherine ignored this and in December 1560 went ahead and married Edward Seymour, 1st Earl of Hertford, son of the Duke of Somerset, in secret and unwitnessed. Elizabeth, unaware of the marriage, sent Edward abroad in a bid to widen his horizons and improve his education while Katherine was pregnant with the couple's first child, a fact she managed to keep secret for almost eight months.

Left with nowhere to turn, Katherine looked to Sir Robert Dudley for help, asking him to intercede on her behalf with Elizabeth, which he agreed to do. He told the queen everything he knew of Katherine's predicament the day after; she was furious and sent Katherine to the Tower, where her husband was to join her on his return. Once again Elizabeth felt this was all part of a wider conspiracy to take her crown and was determined to make an example of her cousin. Katherine was kept in comfortable surroundings and gave birth to her son Edward there in 1561. By the terms of Henry VIII's will, this little boy was technically next in line for the throne. Thanks to the kindness of Sir Edward Werner, Lieutenant of the Tower, he allowed the married couple to secretly meet – this turned out to be a very reckless move as she fell pregnant again and gave birth to her second son, Thomas, in 1563. When Elizabeth heard of this, she was apoplectic with rage and ordered Katherine to be permanently separated from her husband and eldest son. Following her release from the Tower she was moved among various noblemen who took custody of her, she remained under house arrest until she died at the age of just twenty-seven in 1568. The marriage was eventually annulled by the archbishop of Canterbury, making the children illegitimate and therefore no threat to the throne. She was initially laid to rest at Yoxford Church in Suffolk before being reinterred next to her husband at Salisbury Cathedral following his death in 1621 at the grand age of eighty-one.

Katherine's younger sister Mary fared no better when it came to incurring Elizabeth's wrath as she too married without royal consent. She secretly wed Thomas Keyes, a man of no great noble lineage, clearly not wanting to make the same mistake as Katherine, the ceremony was attended by three witnesses. The match was considered unsuitable in many ways, Thomas was much older than Mary and had been married before – he had been widowed and had several children. It was not just dynastic issues the couple faced, there were also physical difficulties to be overcome. He was a massive 6ft 8in tall and she was described as being 'crook-backed', 'very ugly' and short, maybe not even topping 5ft, they were mercilessly mocked by the court so it is no wonder they kept their relationship under wraps. The unlikely couple married on 16 July 1565 but when Elizabeth discovered the marriage had taken place Keyes was arrested and placed in the Fleet Prison, they would never see each other again. He was not released until 1569, at which time Mary was considered the true heir to the throne following her sister's death, she was placed under house arrest and sent to live with Sir Thomas Gresham. Like her sister she was moved among various noble families but unlike Katherine, Mary managed to redeem herself and eventually became one of Elizabeth's maids of honour. Mary died aged 33 and is buried in Westminster Abbey.

But what did Katherine's and Mary's fall from grace mean to the Lennox family and their claim to the throne? Well, quite a bit in terms of how Elizabeth saw them, she decided to pardon them for their supposed crimes and release them from their house arrest. She told the couple she had forgiven them and forgotten their offence but she refused to have Margaret or Lennox admitted to her presence. It would appear that Elizabeth's newfound dislike of Katherine Grey bolstered Margaret's position, although she had been required to swear the oath. They may have been granted their freedom but all the hard work they had put in prior to their incarceration had been obliterated, their network of spies had gone and it would take time to rebuild the connections. In order to do this, they returned to the safety of the north and to Settrington, but when they arrived, they found their beloved home almost in ruins; it appeared to have been ransacked with many of their belongings stolen by opportunists who found the house unguarded.

It appears Elizabeth soon had a change of heart and requested Margaret join her at court. She was not ready to bring Lennox back, but she had her troublesome cousin under her watchful gaze, it must have seemed to all that Margaret was back in high favour. With this latest imprisonment came the realisation for Margaret that she would never inherit the English throne and in that realisation came the moment she and Lennox decided to focus their aims on Darnley. It would be through him the thrones would unite and she set to work in establishing how she would go about this. She reached out to Francis Yaxley, a member of parliament at the English court, and tasked him with unearthing any other suitors that Mary might have had, including Don Carlos of Portugal.

It was around this time in 1563 that Margaret commissioned a full-length portrait of her sons. Despite a distinct lack of funds, money was found to pay Flemish artist Hans Eworth to paint the seventeen-year-old Darnley and his younger brother Charles. In it, Darnley stands with a white handkerchief and a pair of gloves in his left hand while his right hand is placed affectionately on his younger brother's shoulder. They are both dressed head to toe in black, Darnley wears a tight-fitting doublet which displays his lean legs and a pure white ruff around his collar showing off his handsome face. Charles is aged 6 and is dressed in skirts as was the norm for boys his age (boys were usually 'breeched' between the ages of 4 and 8 years old.) The Lennoxes were clever in commissioning this painting at this time, it is a statement piece and shows Darnley as a virile young man who is ripe for marriage. The painting is currently in the care of the Royal Collection and is on display in Mary, Queen of Scots' bedchamber at the Palace of Holyroodhouse in Edinburgh.

By mid-1563, Elizabeth was ready once again to accept both Margaret and Lennox back to court and they took Darnley with them. He was fast becoming a favourite of Elizabeth's, he would play the lute and sing for her. It was felt enough time had passed and the Lennoxes had clearly had been behaving themselves, Cecil's spies had nothing to report so now seemed an ideal opportunity to bring them back into the fold. Elizabeth even went as far as writing to Queen Mary in Scotland requesting the attainder against Lennox be dropped and his title and estates returned to him. It is unclear why she has this sudden change of heart at this particular time, she had previously abandoned any notion of helping them, so why now? One suggestion is that Elizabeth was hoping they would return to Scotland and that Margaret would all of a sudden become a problem for Mary rather than herself, although that seems a very risky move to make because while they were in England they could be kept under surveillance, whereas if they were to reside in Scotland they could have openly plotted with Mary. On the other hand, this could be seen as an empty gesture with Elizabeth knowing full well that Mary would not want to have to deal with Margaret and the ongoing saga over the Angus and Lennox titles and lands and so would decline the request.

South of the border the English courtiers concerned themselves over the succession, while north of the border there was still the question of who Queen Mary was to marry. Talk of a union with Don Carlos was still rife but Elizabeth had her own ideas. She had many suggestions of potential English bridegrooms for Mary to marry, including her favourite, Lord Robert Dudley, although he was far below Mary in rank. Elizabeth stipulated that if she let Mary pick her future husband, she would then make her the heir to the crown of England. Elizabeth was playing games; she would not reveal outright the identity of her proposed grooms as it was in her best interests to keep Mary dangling as long as possible. This meant she could stall her from marrying anyone. Elizabeth had a complicated outlook on marriage – which is understandable given her family history; she refused to be drawn on the subject, to her she was the lawful queen and was not willing to place the English crown on the head of a foreign prince or an English nobleman. Ironically, she felt it her place to meddle in the marital affairs of her Scottish counterpart when really, she should not have been intervening at all.

It took until March 1564 for Elizabeth to officially offer Dudley as a potential husband for Mary but his lowly state led Mary to refuse him, she saw him as nothing more than Elizabeth's servant (he served as Master of the Horse). It seems a strange offer to make, Mary did not want to marry him, he did not want to marry Mary and Elizabeth did not want him to leave England – again Elizabeth is making empty gestures, second guessing what Mary's response would be, this time she guessed correctly. Mary knew she had to play the long game, she understood the need to keep Elizabeth happy in order to maintain her position as heir to the throne so took her time to reveal her position, she was keeping her options open and keeping Elizabeth on tenterhooks.

Great news arrived for Lennox in late April 1564, Mary decided to restore him to his titles and estates and invited him to return to Scotland in order for her to officially reinstate him to his rightful position. Naturally, Elizabeth was not keen in letting Lennox head north and initially refused permission for him to travel; was she worried this was Mary hinting that Darnley was her preferred option as a husband? It seems perfectly plausible, given that Margaret had already formally suggested Darnley as a husband for Mary and this news quickly got back to Cecil and Elizabeth. In a surprise move the queen eventually agreed for Lennox to return to Scotland, albeit reluctantly, but how could she openly refuse the request of another monarch without revealing her hand? Unfortunately, when Margaret requested permission to take both of their sons with them, Elizabeth refused point blank and withdrew the travel licence, she felt they had no need to accompany their father and wrote to Mary requesting she refuse Lennox access to Scotland should he, or any member of his family, attempt to enter the country. Mary saw no issue with allowing him to travel and eventually Elizabeth had no option but to relent on the understanding he did not do anything that could potentially harm England and her interests in Scotland. Knowing of Elizabeth's ability to change her mind at any time, Lennox left almost immediately, leaving Margaret and his sons behind, he arrived in Edinburgh on 23 September. Once again, the couple were forced into a prolonged separation, although neither could have predicted the events that would happen before they were to be reunited again. His mission in the first instance was to befriend the queen and try to establish some kind of connection with her, it was hoped by doing so he would gain some kind of influence over her decisions, especially those she was making about her future husband. Having Lennox at court would have been a constant reminder to her of Darnley, while other suitors offered their hands, he could not have been far from her thoughts.

While Lennox was away, life for Margaret carried on as normal and on 6 July 1564, she and Elizabeth both stood as godmother at the christening of Cecil's daughter Elizabeth. Despite Cecil's spy network set up to work against her, Margaret maintained a good relationship with the queen's chief advisor and would often turn to him for help. She recognised how influential he was with the queen and so always remained on good terms with him, he interceded with

Elizabeth on numerous occasions, offering a more logical approach rather than an emotional one.

The tables turned fast for Lennox; he was no longer considered a traitor in Scotland after Mary had managed to persuade the Scottish nobles to accept him back. All of a sudden, he became a high-ranking noble who was in high favour with the queen. But Mary was wary of Lennox as was her half-brother, James Stewart, Earl of Moray – the illegitimate son of James V, he would be at Mary's side throughout most of her reign in Scotland, often as support but also as an enemy. He remembered Lennox's betrayal when he had led English forces against the Scots and was adamant he should not have his titles and estates returned to him, let alone his son be considered as a groom for Mary. Aware of the opposition he faced, Lennox set about gathering his allies around him. He turned to his kinsman the Earl of Atholl, and along the way recruited the Earls of Caithness, Eglinton and Lord Livingston to name just a few. They were all aware of the plot to marry Darnley to Mary and all supported the cause.

If Mary was considering Darnley as a prospective husband, then his father could not be an exiled traitor so it made sense for her to restore him. She kept to her word and on 14 October 1564, twenty-six years after he was stripped of his title and lands, he was proclaimed at the Mercat Cross in Edinburgh and formerly restored to them, officially making Margaret the Countess of Lennox. He was granted the best apartments at Holyrood Palace but a marriage could not take place while Darnley was in England so they now faced the tricky task of getting him north of the border and into Mary's world. Ambassador Sir James Melville was sent south to London in a bid to persuade Elizabeth to let Darnley travel, the pretext was that he was needed in Scotland to secure his father's reinstatement, as his heir it was deemed necessary for him to be part of the negotiations; Melville was then to bring Darnley home to England once the political side of things were taken care of. With Melville away at the English court, Margaret made her intentions for her son clear to him: he was to marry the queen no matter the cost to her, she was sacrificing her freedom for the good of his advancement and that was seen as a sacrifice worth making.

When Melville returned to Scotland he took with him Margaret's lavish gifts for himself, the queen and Lennox. Elizabeth was still blindly clinging to the idea of Mary marrying Dudley, and in order to help change the queen's mind she created him the Earl of Leicester in a ceremony in September 1564 at which Darnley carried the Sword of State in front of the queen. What Elizabeth failed to realise was that Dudley had no interest in marrying Mary, the promise of a crown was not enough to tempt him away from England, or Elizabeth. Instead, he did his best, along with Cecil and Margaret, to help convince Elizabeth that sending Darnley to Scotland was the right thing to do. She had gone to great lengths to include Darnley in court matters, including making him part of the welcoming party for the new Spanish ambassador Guzman de Silva who arrived in the country in the June of 1564. It was good timing for Margaret as no doubt his arrival at court was beneficial in discussions surrounding Darnley's marriage – the Spanish were still keen for this union to go ahead as they were potential Catholic allies. It took some careful persuasion, but she eventually relented and granted Darnley a licence to travel north to join up with his father.

At the time Darnley left London in January 1565 Margaret was in high favour; he was given permission to stay for three months at which point he was to return to England bringing his father with him, to stay any longer would have been an outright dismissal of Queen Elizabeth's orders. Having to say goodbye to Lennox just a few months before would have been difficult for Margaret but to say goodbye to her most treasured son must have been a real wrench for her. He was not politically adept and lacked any kind of common sense so Margaret had to impress upon him that it was his duty to marry Queen Mary, it was what the family had been working towards and they now finally had the opportunity to bring it about. The problem was that for all his education, Darnley was spoilt and immature; Margaret and Lennox had made him the centre of their world for so long he was used to having everything revolve around him. He was ill equipped to rule, he was headstrong and ambitious but did not use those traits as well as his mother did. He was keen to become a king but did not relish the hard work that went with it and Margaret must have worried how he was going to fare in Scotland. Little did either of them know that when she waved him off on his travels, they would never see each other again.

Around this time Margaret commissioned the beautiful Lennox Jewel, sometimes known as the Darnley Jewel. It is believed the jewel was commissioned as a token of her love for her husband but it can also be seen as statement of power and nobility. It is thought she probably requested it to be made when Lennox was in Scotland fighting to win back his title just before Darnley's marriage to the queen, although when it was made and its exact message is open to debate.

The gold locket is an intricate heart shape that measures around three inches in length and is encrusted with various gemstones and enamel depicting symbols of Lennox and Angus power. The front of the locket shows the figures of Faith, Hope, Victory and Truth surrounding a winged heart which is set with a large polished blue glass stone, possibly a sapphire. These figures are representative of Margaret's Catholic faith, and of hers and Matthew's hopes for Darnley. Around the rim of the locket is a white enamel border with the motto: QVHA. HOPIS. STIL. CONSTANLY. VITH PATIENCE SAL. OBTEAIN. VICTORIE. IN YAIR. PRETENCE (Who hopes still constantly with patience shall obtain victory in their claim). This can be interpreted to mean the right to the crowns of England and Scotland and their belief of their dynastic right to both. Above the blue heart Victory and Truth hold a crown set with three rubies and a table-cut emerald set underneath. The crown opens up to reveal two hearts that have been pierced by two arrows, presumably shot by Cupid and the motto: QUAT WE RESESOLV (What we resolve). The combination of hearts and crown were symbols of the Douglas clan. Above the blue heart are the engraved initials MSL for Matthew and Margaret Stewart Lennox which are crowned by a wreath, a sign of everlasting love. A winged heart opens up to reveal the device of two clasped hands and a green hunting horn surrounded by the inscription: DEATHE SAL DESOLVE (Death shall dissolve); below this device is rather macabre skull and crossbones which is there to remind the wearer of their own mortality and also again of the undying love of Matthew and Margaret.

The reverse of the locket has numerous religious emblems on a gold background, including a glorious sun amid a star-studded azure sky. In the corner is a crescent moon, a sign of rebirth/resurrection, with a male face in profile. A crowned salamander, Margaret's own device, triumphantly emerges from fire unscathed, a reference to her own survival from the difficulties she had faced. Below is a pelican in her piety, feeding her young with blood from its own breast. A strong symbol of maternal sacrifices and a nod towards Margaret's role as a mother, she suffered much heartache in losing six of her children in infancy and a reminder that she is willing to sacrifice herself and her freedom for the advancement of her son. The figure of a man reclining on grass could either be Lennox or Darnley, he is surrounded by a crown and has a sunflower bursting upwards symbolising his royal authority and that of Christ. Surrounded by the motto: MY STAIT TO YIR I MAY COMPAER FOR ZOV QVHA IS OF BONTES RAIR (My state to these I may compare for you who are of rare goodness).

The back of the jewel opens up to reveal a stake among flames, more than likely a religious martyr symbolising Margaret's own battles for her religion. A queen sits on her throne with the motto: GAR TEL. MY. RELAES (Cause tell my release) on a scroll above her which may refer to Margaret's recent release from the Tower of London, although the fact the figure is crowned may be in reference to Queen Mary. The figure of Time with cloven feet like the devil holds an hour-glass in its left hand and extends its right hand to a naked female figure in a pool of water, with scrolls bearing mottos: TYM. GARES AL LEIR (Time causes all to learn). Now was the time for the Lennoxes to act and time was against them. On a scroll above Time is the motto ZE SEIM. AL MY. PLESVR (You seem all my pleasure) below it is the mouth of hell where fire and demons are projected out. Further down are two men: an armed soldier and his slain enemy, both are wearing classical armour, the fallen man is pointing to a red shield by his side and a crowned warrior, possibly Darnley, is holding a female figure by the hair, his sword is drawn as if he is about to slay her. It is unsure if this in relation to Darnley or Lennox.

The jewel was meant to be worn as a pendent around the neck and uses sixteenth-century Scots language. It is not known with absolute certainty when it was made, there are arguments for it being prior to Darnley's marriage but others suggest it may have been after Lennox's death. It is a jewel that encapsulates love and devotion both to each other and to their dynastic aspirations. It is a jewel not without controversy but it is also a heartfelt tribute to the love shared between Margaret and Matthew and their hope for the future of their son. Regardless of its true origins it is a beautifully crafted piece of jewellery that has clearly been given and received in love; it is currently in the care of the Royal Collection.

Chapter 14

The Marriage of Lord Darnley and Mary, Queen of Scots

Elizabeth seems to have a huge change of heart when it comes to Darnley marrying Mary. She does offer Dudley and the Duke of Norfolk as alternatives, but encouraged by Cecil and Dudley she allows Darnley to travel to Scotland. The pretence could have been that he was travelling for political reasons on behalf of his father, but Elizabeth must have anticipated he would be negotiating a marriage with the queen. This sudden change of heart could be for a number of reasons; there is the issue of religion for one thing, by marrying a Catholic to a Catholic she may have hoped it would bring division to Scotland and cause further rifts among Calvinists and Catholics, which would cause Mary problems. She might also have assumed that Darnley would do nothing to put his claim to the English throne in jeopardy by marrying without royal assent, even if he had not considered the impact the marriage would have on his claim, then surely Margaret would have. But just like his mother, Darnley was not going to let royal permission stand in his way, and neither was the threat of losing lands and properties in England an obstacle that could not be overcome.

For Elizabeth, there were some advantages to Mary marrying Darnley – for one, it would ensure she did not make an alliance with a foreign superpower, a union with Catholic Spain would have been a disaster for England. Darnley's character was another factor that Elizabeth might have taken into consideration. He was known for being proud, spoilt and selfish and she probably realised that he could cause Mary more problems than he would solve, and given

Cecil's political know-how it seems unthinkable that he would advise Elizabeth to let Darnley go without having a plan in place. The English councillors were playing a very risky game, but as Mary had granted Darnley permission to enter Scotland, Elizabeth was left with no choice but to agree. The uniting of two legitimate claimants to the throne does seem a bizarre decision to make but technically, by the law of the day, Mary had no claim to the English throne by the very fact she was Scottish. As for Darnley, Margaret's heirs had been barred from ascending the throne by the Act of Succession anyway, so his claim was tenuous at best. Elizabeth would have to hope that if the need came, the Protestant lords of England would unite against Catholic rule and protect her throne.

Darnley finally arrived in Scotland in February 1565. His first stop was Holyrood where he waited for his father to arrive; Lennox had been at Dunkeld with the Earl of Atholl no doubt plotting on his behalf. From Holyrood father and son rode down to Wemyss Castle in Fife where the court was currently assembled. When he arrived on 17 February Darnley presented himself to the queen and made an instant impression on her. Melville describes Mary's first thoughts when seeing Darnley, gone was the lanky 14-year-old lad: 'Her majesty took well with him, and said that he was the lustiest and best proportioned long man that she had ever seen; for he was of high stature, long and small, even and erect.' Both Mary and Darnley were young, beautiful and tall – standing at just over 6ft they towered over everyone around them; soon after his arrival, however, Darnley became ill with a bout of smallpox, or more likely syphilis. Mary spent a lot of time visiting him, which for an anointed queen was a risk given he could have been infectious; not to be deterred by this, she brushed those fears aside and continued to nurse him. While his own mother languished in London, Mary took on mothering duties and nursed Darnley back to health. It was during this time her feelings for Darnley grew, it was clear an attachment was forming between them and by the time he left his sick bed Mary was enamoured by him.

Darnley was making a good impression; it seems he could turn on the charm when it pleased him and before long, he was winning over some of Scotland's more defiant nobles. Gone for the time being was the proud and arrogant young man and in his place was a likeable fellow who Randolph described as being 'courteous dealing with all men deserves great praise and is well spoken of'. It would appear Darnley had pulled the wool over many people's eyes since his arrival in Scotland, no doubt he had been grilled by his mother before leaving England in how to behave.

His good behaviour even led to Moray coming around to the idea of him and Mary marrying. As his stock rose in favour, Darnley made sure he was never far from Mary's side, he was enjoying everything her court had to offer. They enjoyed dancing together and spent time playing cards and dice with one another – but when Darnley proposed, she refused him; surprisingly, it was her ministers that persuaded Mary to accept him. At this stage, Robert Dudley, the newly created Earl of Leicester, was still in the frame as a prospective husband, but Mary wanted reassurances that she would be named as Elizabeth's heir if she agreed to the match; Elizabeth told Mary she could only do this once she herself had either married or declared she would not. This was enough to turn Mary away from any possible marriage with Dudley, and when the option of marrying Don Carlos came to an end due to rumours of madness, that just left Darnley.

The decision had been made and before long Mary was seeking advice from her councillors over a potential marriage to Darnley. Unfortunately, Darnley could not keep up the pretence of being pleasant for long enough and Moray was soon having doubts, advising Mary not to wed the tempestuous English lord. When she ignored his advice, he left court in disgust and began to rally his supporters. Support for Moray began to grow; Darnley was gaining a reputation more akin to his true personality and many of Scotland's lords began to vocalise their opposition to the marriage. There was still some support for the marriage however, the Lennox supporters still championed the idea as did Mary's secretary David Rizzio, who looked to self-promotion should the match succeed. He began to infiltrate Mary's relationship with Moray, working at putting a divide between them and constantly putting pressure on her to remove Moray's power. Moray knew full well that if Darnley became king, his power would be all but over – he turned to Elizabeth for help and she obliged by sending funds.

Lennox was also moving his men in; Atholl began to take more control over the government and slowly but surely the old guard were out and the Lennox-approved guard were in. As the political wrangles wore on Mary was slowly becoming more and more infatuated with Darnley, she quite clearly refused to listen to her ministers who urged her to see his true character, which was now at its petulant best. His violent tempers were becoming more frequent and were likely caused by syphilis, a disease he probably first contracted while in France. Mary continued to shower Darnley with expensive gifts, she pampered his ego and over time she disregarded the thoughts of anyone else in terms of whether this was a good marriage to make. She loved Darnley and was going to marry him and no man or woman was going to come in the way of that. She disregarded her ministers' pleas to see his true character and Elizabeth's approval no longer mattered, although Mary could argue the fact Elizabeth had let him travel to Scotland, so in a way had given her approval.

It shocked many that Mary had been taken in by Darnley, they were surprised she could not see what his true character was like but she had been blinded by his good looks and the smooth words he no doubt dripped into her ears when they were alone. All Darnley had to do was convince Mary that he was the perfect choice to become her husband and king to Scotland, what the ministers thought really was of no concern to him, he disregarded their thoughts and probably convinced Mary too. Once again Scotland stood on the brink of destruction, torn in two by warring factions that could not agree on how, or by whom, the country should be governed. Many felt, and hoped, the queen would come to her senses and listen to her council; they continued to urge her to turn away from the match but she was in too deep now – whatever Darnley did or said to her worked, she was under his spell. Her queenly reputation was under threat, since her return from France she had cleverly negotiated government and dealt with Knox and the religious upheaval well but all that was now under threat due to an inability to listen to reason. Just like her grandmother Margaret Tudor, it would appear Mary let affairs of the heart cloud her judgement. On the one hand it is admirable that these two queens took their destiny into their own hands, but in the sixteenth century, women who thought they knew what was best for them, let alone the country, were not liked. Mary stood on the threshold of disaster and, blinded by love, she moved ever closer to her destruction.

Aware that Elizabeth's agreement to the marriage would be needed for diplomatic reasons, Mary sent her secretary William Maitland to London to request permission for Darnley to marry her. Elizabeth and Cecil realised their mistake in allowing Darnley to visit Scotland. Elizabeth had hoped that by marrying Dudley to Mary she could control the Scottish throne, but she had been out manoeuvred when Mary insisted she would not marry him – much to his relief. Elizabeth was angry with Darnley for shirking his sense of honour, in her eyes he should have been the one asking permission, he was her subject and should have travelled to England to face his sovereign. But as it was fast becoming apparent, Darnley was a coward and was not going to take the risk of being held prisoner; he was happy to leave that fate to his mother, who instantly fell from grace once the news of the intended marriage reached the queen's ears. Elizabeth placed Margaret under house arrest and ordered her to keep to her apartments at Whitehall while they awaited further news from Scotland. Margaret tried all she could to convince Elizabeth she knew nothing of the marriage plan but that was never going to be believed, Margaret was not the kind of woman, or mother, that would not be aware of what was happening in her son's life. Elizabeth ignored Margaret's pleas and ordered Lennox and Darnley home to England; they outright refused and Mary gave them leave to remain safely in Scotland under her protection. Angered by their defiance and Margaret's supposed ignorance, Elizabeth sent her Scottish ambassador Nicholas Throckmorton to Edinburgh to discover more details and to put a stop to the marriage. He discovered that many of the Scottish lords were against the marriage too.

When support for the marriage was not forthcoming from England, Mary turned to the Catholic heads of state in Europe for approval and they willingly supported the match without fully understanding what kind of character Darnley had; England was being out voted. Back home in Scotland there was still a distinct split between those who supported the match, led by Lennox, and those against it, led by Moray. The support of Moray was important for Mary, up to now he had used a difference of religious opinions as his reasoning for not supporting the marriage, Moray was a leading Protestant among the Lords of the Congregation (a group of nobles who supported the reformation in Scotland) and did not relish Mary marrying another Catholic. Mary would never waver on the issue of her religion and looked to reassure Moray that Darnley would not receive the Crown Matrimonial due to his age, but this was not enough and he still refused to support his sister. While Mary tried her best to deal with the political side of things Darnley continued to be insolent and rude, seemingly not understanding the perilous situation developing around him.

On 10 June Darnley was created Earl of Ross and swore his allegiance to Mary. This was a pivotal moment; up to that moment he had been a subject of Elizabeth's and had sworn allegiance to her, but by taking this new oath he was openly turning his back on her and by doing so placed his mother in extreme danger. Being created an earl was not enough to satisfy Darnley's desire for power, he wanted and expected a dukedom to be conferred on him and when that was not forthcoming, he got angry and lashed out. His behaviour was becoming more and more erratic, he would spend time in the brothels and inns of Edinburgh, getting so drunk he could not find his way home to Holyrood. With more erratic behaviour came more warnings for Mary, her Guise relatives in France had heard of Darnley's antics and urged her to call off the wedding, his behaviour was becoming hard to ignore and even harder to defend, but defend him she did.

Things were getting desperate, many plans were made to bring things to a halt, including a plot led by Moray and funded by Elizabeth to kidnap Darnley and Lennox and return them to England, but it all came to nothing when Mary heard news of the plans. But what of Lennox, where was he in all this? He quite clearly could not control his wayward son, he appears to have been powerless to bring him to heel which begs the question: how would Darnley have behaved if his mother had been present? It is hard to imagine Margaret would have stood for this kind of behaviour from her son, she was too shrewd and wily to let his behaviour destroy all they had worked for. She would have seen the damage he was doing to their hopes and put a stop to it, unfortunately, she was in London and in no position to help.

Mary was clearly paving the way to marry the man she loved, regardless of what her nobles thought. But what exactly were the issues with Darnley? He certainly came from good stock, he had royal blood from both countries in his veins, and he was well educated and handsome. Unfortunately, he was insufferably proud and his rise to an earldom made him even more so, he started to overreach himself and began to openly criticise Elizabeth seemingly without any thought to his mother who was at the queen's mercy. It is not difficult to understand why Darnley was disliked by so many for his attitudes and behaviour and he did nothing to try to mend his tarnished reputation, knowing full well that he was on the verge of becoming king. Like his mother all those years before, he believed himself invincible; he knew he had the love of the queen which made him untouchable and as long as she remained besotted with him, he could continue to behave in any way he pleased. He was ambitious and power hungry, unfortunately he was not the kind of person that could wield that power effectively.

But Darnley did have one weapon in his armoury: his mother. Margaret may have been languishing under house arrest far away in London but it did not stop her doing all she could to garner support where she could. In the first instance she reached out to Morton and advised him she would give up her claim to the Angus titles and estates in return for his backing and support of the marriage. It was his nephew Archibald who had become the new Earl of Angus, but due to his infancy Morton collected the monies due from the estates. With Margaret ceasing her claim, he could go on unopposed. Morton readily agreed and lent his support to the marriage. This is a prime example of Margaret's influence in Scottish affairs. Despite being incarcerated miles away she could still successfully negotiate political dealings, she commanded the respect of a lot of the Scottish nobles and many of them may have reluctantly supported Darnley out of respect for her. Slowly but surely more Scottish lords came over to Mary and Darnley's side and when she formally asked for their support in light of Elizabeth's refusal, they agreed. Many took offence that England was trying to assert its influence in Scottish politics, patriotism came before anything else and they backed their queen – except Moray, he still refused to support the match so took himself away from court and the council, leading the way for Lennox's ally Atholl to take the reins of government.

With confirmation from Throckmorton that the marriage was going ahead Elizabeth prepared to make her move against Margaret. Her imprisonment all of a sudden became much stricter; on 16 June 1565 she was to leave the comfort of Whitehall and enter the Tower of London as a prisoner for the second time in her life. She was accompanied by six guards and Sir Francis Knollys, Elizabeth's vice chamberlain, and was permitted to take just three of her women. They all sailed by barge up the Thames to the formidable fortress, which they entered through Traitor's Gate, from there they were taken to the Lieutenant's house which overlooked Tower Green. Did Margaret feel fear as she gazed out over the execution site of Anne Boleyn and Catherine Howard, or did she assume her rank would save her, again? Due to her status, she would be lodged in relative comfort but she was to be allowed no visitors; all of a sudden, her lines of communication with Scotland were severely restricted and all she could do was sit and anxiously wait for news. By holding Margaret prisoner Elizabeth hoped to lure Lennox and Darnley back to England, but she underestimated just how much the Lennoxes wanted this match. No doubt Margaret had given instructions they were to stay in Scotland at all costs, she had worked too hard for this to falter when they were so close. She must have anticipated what Elizabeth would do when the plot was discovered but put her faith in the belief that the punishment would go no further than imprisonment. Elizabeth did go a step further, she seized Temple Newsam which reverted to the crown leaving Margaret under severe financial pressure, while young Charles was sent back into the care of the Archbishop of York, separated once again from his mother.

When Queen Mary heard of Margaret's imprisonment she was horrified, so much so she sent her Master of Requests, John Hay, to England to argue that the severity of the punishment was too harsh and that Elizabeth should give Margaret her liberty – after all, what had she done wrong? It is not as though she was in Scotland personally negotiating her son's marriage, that had been down to Lennox. But Elizabeth needed to have some leverage against her rival queen and the only way she could do that was to hold Margaret prisoner in the hope it would force Darnley into calling off the nuptials. Alongside Mary's pleas were those of Spain, they had made their position clear early on that they supported the marriage and to hear Margaret was imprisoned would have sat uncomfortably with them. When it seemed nothing was working, Mary wrote to King Charles IX, her former brother-in-law in France, asking for his support. He agreed and wrote to Elizabeth to intercede on Margaret's behalf, but she was too enraged to take any notice. Unfortunately, these petitions did more harm than good for they indicated there was a potential Catholic plot to remove Elizabeth from her throne and she was not willing to risk giving Margaret her freedom to continue plotting on her son's behalf. The requests inadvertently caused Margaret's imprisonment to become more severe and she spent her fiftieth birthday confined in the Tower of London, far away from her family and supporters.

Despite Margaret's imprisonment the marriage between Mary, Queen of Scots and Henry, Lord Darnley, took place in the early hours of 29 July 1565 in the private chapel at the Palace of Holyroodhouse. She had earlier created him the Duke of Albany and had him proclaimed King Henry of Scotland, although she still refused to grant her new husband the Crown Matrimonial due to his relatively young age. When he was proclaimed, there was a lone voice in the crowd that rejoiced in replying 'God save the King', that voice belonged to his father Lennox; the rest of the nobility stood silent, this marriage was not well received.

When the news reached Margaret in London she rejoiced in her prison, all her best laid plans had finally come to fruition, her precious son had succeeded in marrying the queen of Scotland and her master plan of uniting the thrones of England and Scotland had moved a significant step closer. But Elizabeth was seething, it appeared she had been duped and by letting Lennox and Darnley visit Scotland she had in effect handed Darnley to Mary on a silver platter. A betrayal like this was not going to pass without further restrictions being imposed on the Lennoxes, Elizabeth was determined to make them pay. Settrington was seized and at Temple Newsam an inventory was made of all its valuables and a note made of the rents they received from all their properties. With all sources of income now stopped in England, the worry of how she was going to pay for her upkeep in prison was a cause for concern. She was generously given clothes and furniture from the royal stores and her servants' wages were paid by Elizabeth, but Margaret would have to repay her and with little or no income this was going to prove very difficult. Luckily, following a full assessment of her assets, the Lennoxes were permitted to keep Temple Newsam and Settrington but all their other estates were seized by the crown and sold off, with the proceeds going to repay any debts that were outstanding.

Seizing property and land was one way of punishing Margaret, but there was one more tactic Elizabeth had up her sleeve. Darnley may be on the throne of Scotland, but the Lennoxes did have another son

Elizabeth could take control of. Charles was just eight years old when his mother was taken to the Tower, he was placed in the care of the Archbishop of York but was allowed to remain living at Settrington which would have been familiar and offered some comfort to him. Like his mother, he was kept under strict surveillance as the estate lay just thirty miles from the Yorkshire coast and there were genuine concerns a rescue attempt from Scotland could be launched. He may only have been a young boy at this time but Charles was a Catholic male with Tudor royal blood in his veins and would have been seen as a good match for any Catholic monarch with a marriageable daughter, a marriage that could bring further strife to England. How had it got to this? How had England allowed one family to hold so much power they could potentially bring the monarchy to its knees? As with many things during this period religion played a big part, had the Lennox family been Protestants no one would have looked to them to lead a potential rebellion, but their Catholicism meant they offered an appealing alternative option. The Catholic royal powerhouses of France and Spain wanted England to return to Rome to help in the fight against Protestantism that swept across Europe, and when Elizabeth was excommunicated by a Papal Bull issued by Pope Pius V in February 1570 on the grounds of heresy, it gave Catholics the authority to rise against her and remove her from the throne without fear of retribution in the eyes of God. Much to Spain and France's dismay the people of England remained loyal to their queen and did not rise against her and with that Protestantism became the established religion of England.

In the end no one did try to rescue Charles and he seems to have been left to cope without either parent or his elder brother. It is not known how well he was treated by his guardians but one can only assume he was well taken care of as Elizabeth would not want any further scandal linked to one of the Lennox sons. It is hard not to feel some kind of sympathy for the young boy, his happiness and security seems to have been sacrificed for the good of his elder brother. When Margaret and Lennox were plotting for this marriage, they may have readily accepted it would not be without risks for them, but did they consider the risks that could be involved for Charles? He was just an innocent child caught up in his parents' and elder sibling's desire for greatness. He would not have known if or when he would see any of his family again.

While Margaret spent her birthday in the Tower, Darnley was becoming increasingly insufferable north of the border. Not even Lennox could get through to him or control his increasingly wayward son, he wrote to Margaret on 19 December:

> My Meg, we have to give God most hearty thanks for
> that the king our son continues in good health and liking,
> and the queen great with child, God save them all, for
> the which we have great cause to rejoice more. Yet of my
> part, I must confess I want and find a lack of my chiefest
> comfort, which is you.'

This letter suggest that Lennox either failed to fully understand how disliked his son really was, or that he was protecting Margaret from the truth – that their son's own selfishness and pride would be his downfall. Shortly after their marriage Darnley's attitude towards his wife changed, he became abusive and petulant; sulking over his lack of real power, he felt he was not taken seriously by anyone, including Mary. What he really wanted was the Crown Matrimonial which would have made him co-sovereign with his wife. It would also have meant he could remain on the throne if Mary pre-deceased him – a fact that very few were willing to accept, even Mary saw sense in not granting him this wish. To punish his wife Darnley started having extramarital affairs – even before the honeymoon was over; according to some sources this included liaisons with men. This was strange behaviour even by his standards, he had seen his parents have a happy and stable marriage and there is no suggestion that Lennox ever treated Margaret in any way other than lovingly and with deep respect. Did his upbringing make him so entitled that he could behave in such a callous manner? Maybe the only thing he ever really wanted was the crown, and who could blame him given that from an early age he had been told of his royal lineage and that he had a claim to the throne. It would seem Darnley was a product of his parents' ambitions and things only got worse; he was on the verge of throwing away any power he had as his marriage started to crumble after just five months.

Darnley's true character became apparent to Mary almost immediately after the wedding; his behaviour became even more erratic, he was nasty, shallow and proud, and his anger towards her and her advisors became more and more intense. The fact that Mary was not willing to grant him the Crown Matrimonial demonstrates that her feelings for him quickly began to change; she clearly did not want him to hold any power over her and neither did her advisors, it seems this was one of the few right decisions she made during her reign. From this moment on the marriage seemed destined for failure, they grew further apart and Mary did not want to be in the company of her husband alone, which angered Darnley even more. Before long Darnley was going to find himself out of his depth; never good at diplomacy he was about to walk headlong into a mistake that would see the beginning of the end and put any chance of him wearing the Crown Matrimonial firmly out of the question. It would be one of Mary's closest advisors that would bear the brunt of her rebel lords' anger in the most violent manner and would justify Mary's reasons for having never conferred any further power on her husband. Matters were made yet more delicate as Mary was pregnant with her first child.

Chapter 15

Darnley's Downfall and Margaret's Heartbreak

David Rizzio was born just outside Turin, Italy, in 1533. He was descended from one of Italy's noblest families and became Queen Mary's favourite in around 1561 when he joined her court. Initially he had been employed as the queen's singer and played numerous musical instruments for her pleasure, but things did not stay amicable for long and he was soon making enemies. The queen had lavished fine gifts on him providing him with great wealth and as he rose to become her private secretary in around 1564, the Scottish lords began to feel uneasy as they deemed him to have too much sway over her. Darnley was jealous of the influence Rizzio had over Mary, she seemed to entrust matters of state to him but would not divulge them to Darnley – he even believed that Rizzio was the father of her unborn child. As reckless as always, he got himself involved in a plot with the Protestant lords to murder Rizzio. The plot quickly gained momentum. Darnley was born a Catholic but, like his father, never truly practiced any religion; they seemed able to switch their religious allegiances depending on who they needed to please at the time and so agreed to support the widespread growth of Protestantism across Scotland. One can only imagine what Margaret's response to this would have been, having maintained her Catholic faith through times of great danger she would have been disappointed to see her son be quite willing to dismiss his faith in this way. In return the rebel lords would help Darnley achieve his dream of gaining the Crown Matrimonial by conferring it on him via an act of parliament and, in the process, aid the release of Margaret from the Tower. It is clear to us looking back now that Darnley was being manipulated by the lords; both he and Lennox were naive to believe they would grant this. How much Margaret knew of this plot we do not know, but her husband and eldest son found themselves entangled in a scheme that would have massive repercussions for all those involved.

The fateful day came on 9 March 1566. At around 8.00pm Rizzio was dining with the queen and her ladies in her closet at Holyrood when Darnley joined them. Shortly after, several lords, led by Lord Ruthven, burst into the small room; the heavily pregnant queen was bundled into Darnley's arms and the conspirators demanded Rizzio be handed over to them. A violent struggle then followed, chairs and tables were upended, the queen was terrified, screaming for the lords to stop, she commanded them to leave the chamber at once but they defied her orders. With a loaded gun pointing at her pregnant belly, she must have assumed in that moment the lords had come to kill her. But everything happened so fast and it quickly became apparent they had come for Rizzio. He clung desperately to the queen's skirts, cowering behind her and begging for her to help, but in this situation she was completely powerless to intercede. The lords managed to grab hold of Rizzio and drag him out of the closet into the adjoining bed chamber where they stabbed him fifty-six times. They then proceeded to drag him through the adjacent chambers and out on to the landing, where they threw him down the stairs. Not content with this, they foisted one final act of humiliation on the already dead Rizzio by proceeding to strip his body of his fine jewels and clothes. Darnley's dagger was placed next his body seemingly implicating him in the murder.

The murder of David Rizzio is one of Scottish history's most talked about incidents and there are many rumours surrounding what actually happened that fateful night in Holyrood. Did the queen stand face to face with her lords while one of them aimed a pistol at her? Or was it a knife that one of them drew against their anointed monarch as some have suggested? Whatever the truth, there is no doubt that having to witness such a bloody and brutal attack would have been a terrifying ordeal for the queen and her ladies. It would have been even more shocking to see your husband stand by and let that happen, it must have horrified Mary to know that he was complicit in the attack, as her husband he was bound by honour to protect his wife – even more so given she was heavily pregnant. Rizzio's death is as much a legend as anything else and is marked by a plaque in the Audience Chamber at The Palace of Holyroodhouse. On the floorboard's underneath is a red stain supposedly that of Rizzio's spilled blood. Legends and myths aside, the death of Rizzio was brutal and cowardly; the lords chose to attack him unarmed while at ease with his friends, he may have been a negative influence on the queen but that did not justify the rebel lords' actions. Unfortunately, sixteenth-century Scotland was a brutal place to be and the closer to the throne you were, the greater the risk of being attacked.

Darnley quickly discovered he was way out of his depth and started to lose his nerve, he was not a courageous man and the brutality of the attack shocked and frightened him – if they had done this to Rizzio, could they do it to him too? He knew he was not liked so what would stop them? Would the queen stand by and watch them dispatch him as they had done Rizzio? When the full realisation of what had happened hit him, he began to panic. He soon learned the rebel lords had no intention of keeping to their side of the negotiations and he quickly turned to Mary for help and protection, he had no other option but to throw himself on his wife's mercy and hope she was in a forgiving mood. It was a pitiful sight as he fell to his knees and begged and pleaded with his wife for forgiveness, he insisted he had nothing to do with the lords or their plot to murder Rizzio, but if that was the case why did he not try and prevent the attack? By the accounts given it appears he just stood to one side gripping Mary by the arms to prevent her from moving towards Rizzio. Yes, he was aware of a conspiracy to remove him from the court but he did not think they would go as far as they did or act in such a vicious way.

Always someone who struggled to keep his mouth shut, Darnley went on to tell Mary that the lords planned to keep her under arrest at Stirling Castle for the rest of her life. This idea frightened her but at the same time galvanised her into action, she agreed to forgive her estranged husband and with the help of the Earl of Bothwell they plotted an escape from Holyrood. Mary knew she needed to keep Darnley with her, if left to his own devices he could have created even more damage so she put on a show of reconciliation and unity but the harm was already done; the marriage was over but Mary carried on for the sake of her unborn child. They managed to flee Edinburgh on horseback and made for Dunbar Castle, these scenes are so reminiscent of Margaret Tudor fleeing to safety while heavily pregnant, the events of her grandmother's life often mirrored with Mary's as neither made wise choices in marriage and both were in fear for their lives with a child to protect. But Mary did not have a brother over the border she could turn to for support, instead she had a cold-hearted cousin who was often reluctant to help. Once they reached Dunbar Mary was able to re-establish authority as queen and she was determined to exact revenge on all those involved in Rizzio's murder.

The murder of Rizzio is a pivotal moment in Darnley's life and Mary's reign; the consequences were so far reaching and damaging that they would affect the stability of the country for years to come. From England's perspective, if it had been Elizabeth's intention for Darnley to bring Mary down then she had her wish, but even she could not have anticipated it would have been in such spectacular fashion. Darnley was on a path of self-destruction and as time went on things only got worse, his instability and unpredictable mind made him dangerous. With the help of Bothwell, Mary managed to return to Edinburgh in her capacity as queen, at which point the rebel lords had fled and she had Darnley declared innocent of all wrongdoing, but as with so many decisions in Mary's reign she was soon to discover she had made the wrong one. It did not take long before she learnt the truth of what had happened, and of Darnley and Lennox's involvement in the plot to kill Rizzio.

Far away in London Margaret had to sit in her rooms in the Tower and wait patiently for news, her health was not at its best as the worry and anxiety were starting to take their toll. How much Margaret actually knew of the Rizzio plot beforehand is not clear, if she had been aware she would more than likely have tried to dissuade Lennox from getting involved; yes she was ambitious, but not to the point of murder. Darnley desperately needed the reassuring hand of his mother; Lennox did not seem able to make his son see the errors of his ways, Margaret on the other hand could, she had an air of authority about her that would have brought Darnley to heel. Instead, he was left to be manipulated into agreeing to something he could not see was wrong, both morally and politically. What must have been even more disappointing from Margaret's point of view was that Lennox went along with it; between them they managed to jeopardise everything they had worked so hard to achieve and there was nothing she could do about it.

News from Scotland filtered through and Margaret was aware of Mary's pregnancy, meaning she was able to send her daughter-in-law gifts prior to the birth. Mary set down the terms of the regency should she not survive the birth; it was not uncommon for women to die in childbirth and queens were no different. The plans she laid out did not include Darnley or any member of his family, any favour or trust she had in them had been obliterated. This fact must have devastated Margaret for it was all she had ever dreamed of and now it must have felt like that dream was slowly slipping away.

On 19 June 1566 the queen gave birth to a healthy son at Edinburgh Castle, she named him James. With the birth of James came the security Mary needed, she had secured the succession and now had no need for Darnley. But the new prince had been born into a dangerous era. His mother was clinging to her throne, his father petulantly refused to attend his christening at Stirling Castle and his grandfather, Lennox, was denied all access to him, facts that must have driven Margaret to despair. Despite being imprisoned in the Tower, however, Margaret celebrated the birth of her first grandchild, a child that could one day unite the kingdoms of England and Scotland. James was baptised on 17 December 1566 in the Chapel Royal at Stirling Castle. He had an illustrious set of godparents including Queen Elizabeth, she agreed to stand as godmother to the little prince of Scotland (represented by the Earl of Bedford) and sent him a gold font as a christening gift. Alongside Elizabeth were Charles IX of France (represented by John, Count of Brienne) and Emmanuel Philibert, Duke of Savoy (represented by ambassador Philibert du Croc).

The reports Margaret received from Scotland must have been a great cause for concern for her. She was limited in what she could do given her own dire circumstances, but she was fully aware of the danger her son was in and knew he must try and escape from Scotland in case he was next on the hitlist. Margaret was adept at plotting, especially when it came to her children, and plans were underway to get Darnley and Lennox away from the firepit of Scotland, they had quite clearly outstayed their welcome. They had options, they could sail from the east and follow the coast down as far as Scarborough where he could land and take refuge in the castle and then move onto Settrington and the safety of northern England. The other option was to sail down the west coast and aim to land on the Isles of Scilly which would then provide an excellent departure point for Spain should they feel the need to escape England too. Lennox was not happy with these plans, he thought Darnley should stay in Scotland where his wife and son were, regardless of the fact that his marriage was quite clearly over and access to his son limited. If he was to leave the country altogether it could have been seen as desertion and Mary would have strong grounds on which to divorce her errant husband. Lennox felt so strongly against this idea that he divulged the plot in full to Mary, although once again Darnley denied any knowledge of it and was accused of showing his father a lack of respect. Much to Margaret's disappointment the plan came to nothing and Darnley retreated with his father to Glasgow, the heart of the Lennox lands.

Darnley and Lennox being so far away made Mary uncomfortable; she wanted her husband in Edinburgh where he could be kept under her watchful eye, just in case he decided to get himself embroiled in another ill-advised plot. Although he was so short on allies he would have struggled to do so. Mary needn't have worried; in the January of 1567, Darnley became ill once again and remained in Glasgow on his sick bed, it is noted as being smallpox again although this was probably another bout of syphilis, a disease that seemed to plague Darnley's health. It was only when he was well enough to travel that he was moved closer to Edinburgh, Mary had arranged for him to be brought to Kirk o' Field, just on the outskirts of the city, to convalesce. Margaret learned of her son's illness in a letter that arrived in London around 19 February, little did she know that by then her son was already dead.

Darnley had shown signs of recovery so Mary visited him at the Old Provost's lodging on the evening of 9 February. To any outsider the couple appeared to be fully reconciled with one another, she seemed attentive to him and he appeared to welcome her attentions. She left him to rest just before midnight and returned to Holyrood where she briefly attended a wedding celebration before retiring to her chamber for the evening. In the dead of night, at around 2.00am a huge explosion reverberated around Edinburgh; it was so loud it managed to wake much of the populace, including the queen. The Old Provost's lodging had been blown to pieces by a gunpowder explosion. Initially it was presumed Darnley had perished in the blast but after a thorough search his body could not found in the rubble. The search area was widened and his remains, along with his valet, were found just before dawn in a nearby orchard, approximately 50 yards from the house. Had they been blown from the house as a result of the explosion? It would appear not, he was dressed in just his night gown and there was not a mark upon his body, no sign of gunpowder, no sign of strangulation or of him being involved in a struggle of any kind; clearly, he had not been in the house when it exploded. So how did he die? It would later transpire he had been alerted to a potential attack and decided to flee the house but his would-be attackers chased him down and smothered him, leaving him for dead. It is reported the queen collapsed with grief when she was told the news, but that was nothing compared to the utter devastation Margaret experienced when she was told her eldest son was dead.

When the news finally reached London, Elizabeth was pained to hear that her cousin had been killed in such a way and was adamant that those responsible be punished accordingly. There were also false reports that Lennox had died in the blast, but he was safe in Linlithgow and was still there when he learned of his son's death. But at this stage the belief was that father and son had perished together and Elizabeth had to somehow think of a way to break this news to her cousin. It was a very delicate matter and Elizabeth requested that Margaret Gamage, wife of William Howard, and Mildred Cecil be the ones to tell her. Naturally she was devastated, breaking down when they told her the news that her son was dead at just twenty years old, the manner in which he died must have been incomprehensible. Reports came that, 'The mother was so grieved that it was necessary for the queen to send her doctors to her.' Elizabeth was clearly concerned for Margaret's health, in fact there were genuine concerns Margaret would die from the shock of the news.

In Scotland, a reward of 2,000 crowns was offered to anyone who came forward with information that led to an arrest. It was a substantial reward but answers were needed – and fast, but more importantly, names were needed and the name at the top of the list was the Earl of Bothwell and his known associates. It transpired that he had arranged for the cellar to be packed with gunpowder but he did not actually kill Darnley, the responsibility for that was placed at the feet of the Douglas clan – Margaret's own kinsmen were now being accused of her son's murder. Investigations found that having heard noises from within the house, Darnley grew suspicious and decided to flee with his valet, they managed to climb over a wall and drop into an orchard below before the explosion ripped the house apart. Once the Douglases realised Darnley had fled they chased him down and murdered both him and the valet, it is thought they strangled him with the sleeves of his own night shirt before fleeing into the night. That all seems plausible given the state and positioning of the bodies when they were found but the question on everyone's lips was: how much did Mary know prior to the attack? Many thought she had been given prior knowledge of the attack, Sir Robert Melville arrived in London on 19 February and told the Spanish ambassador, de Silva, that Queen Mary was distressed by what had happened, but also that he suspected 'Queen Mary or her followers had some prior notice of the misfortune'. Even if she had not, it would be difficult to distance herself from the allegations and it would be these allegations that would be the catalyst in Mary's fall. Melville goes on to give a good account of Margaret's reaction when she first learnt of the full goings on at Kirk o' Field, he explains to de Silva that she:

> Used words against his queen, whereat I am nor surprised, as I told him, because grief like this distracts the most prudent people, much more one so sorely beset. She is not the only person that suspects the queen to have had some hand in the business, and they think they see it in revenge for her Italian secretary, and the long estrangement which this caused between her and her husband gave a greater opportunity for evil persons to increase the trouble.

There are some interesting points raised in this. For instance, why was Mary adamant she wanted Darnley in Edinburgh and why lodge him in a house just beyond the city walls? They were estranged and he had little influence to cause a rise against her, so why did she go and visit him that evening – was it to show her consideration, a reconciliation, or maybe it was all part of a plan to make it look like she felt safe enough to visit, knowing what was going to happen later that evening? The idea that this was a revenge attack for Rizzio is very plausible, his murder and the manner of it shocked and devastated her.

Mary did nothing to help allay the suggestion that she was in some way complicit in the murder of her husband, she seemed very reluctant to bring the main suspect, Bothwell, to trial. There was something sinister at the heart of this matter, Bothwell was quite clearly in favour with Mary, he had always been a vocal supporter of hers and she seemed happy to let the perpetrators escape justice. We are told she appeared to be distressed and suffered a mental collapse but her actions did not seem to match her mood. Along with Bothwell, Queen Mary was prime suspect across Europe which unsettled Elizabeth, she felt uneasy that an anointed monarch could be accused in such a way and warned her to take care.

Queen Mary decided to recall Lennox to Edinburgh; he had retreated back to the safety of Glasgow when he heard first the devastating news, but he was hellbent on revenge and arrived back in the capital demanding a trial. He was determined to seek out those responsible and bring them to justice, he claimed he would believe Mary was not involved if she brought Darnley's murderers to justice, and resolved to stay in Scotland until that had been done. Elizabeth had her doubts over Mary's innocence and cooled her correspondence with her, not wanting to become embroiled in such a heinous act. Instead, Elizabeth turned her attentions towards the comfort of Margaret, for which she was praised. She would be further disappointed in Mary when she learnt that Darnley had been buried in Holyrood Abbey without royal honours, he was a member of the English royal family, as well as the Scottish king, and should have been accorded a state funeral as was befitting his status. Was this another hint of Mary's guilt?

It would take until late February for Margaret to learn that her husband was in fact alive. Cecil visited and advised her that Lennox had been in Linlithgow and later Glasgow and was alive and well. Naturally, Margaret was relieved to hear this, but her grief over the loss of Darnley was apparent for Cecil to see and he once again stepped in to help his friend and implored Elizabeth to release Margaret from the Tower. Elizabeth was happy to oblige and arranged for Margaret to be moved to Sackville Place and into the care of Thomas Sackville and his wife. She was to remain under house arrest but the terms of her imprisonment were drastically reduced, she was allowed visitors and Charles was sent for from Yorkshire to join his mother, he was just nine years old at the time of his brother's death and no doubt this reunion was a huge comfort to Margaret.

While Margaret was adjusting to her new accommodation, Lennox continued to fight for justice in Scotland. He persisted in writing to Mary to recall parliament so things could be done in a right and proper manner, it was 14 April before she finally. By dragging her feet, she only reaffirmed suspicions that she had been in some way involved. Lennox demanded that Bothwell in particular be brought to trial but yet again Mary refused, instead she advised Lennox to proceed with a private prosecution, which he did on 24 March when he officially charged Bothwell with the murder of his son and demanded a trial be held before the Estates of Parliament. Bothwell was a powerful man who was quite clearly in favour with Mary and the worries in Edinburgh were that he could easily mount a force that could bring destruction to the city. Soon enough Lennox found himself without support, not necessarily through a dislike of Darnley but simply because the city could not with stand an attack from Bothwell, who had the country's arsenal at his disposal.

Lennox arrived at Linlithgow with 3,000 men at his back, Mary advised him that he could travel on to Edinburgh with only six, whereas Bothwell was granted a total of 400 men. Mary's justification for this is not known, but at the time Scottish law prohibited the accuser to attend a trial armed though she repeatedly seems to back Bothwell against any kind of attack; she is protecting him either out of fear or love. It was clear to all that Mary was not going to sanction a trial so it was felt the best thing Lennox could do was leave Scotland. His time would come but it would not be now, not while men like Bothwell held so much power and sway over the queen.

Meanwhile, in London, Melville went to visit Margaret and found her much calmer than before and she had even cooled in her anger towards Mary. She explained to him that, 'She could not believe that his Queen had been a party to the death of her son, but she could not help complaining of her for her bad treatment of him.' This seems to be a change of heart from Margaret's perspective. Was she softening towards Mary or was this just part of her grieving process? Perhaps she did not believe that anyone would want to harm her son, least of all his wife – the wife Margaret had suggested herself. There may have been an element of regret creeping into her psyche, perhaps she was telling herself it could not be true in a bid to alleviate her own guilt in bringing them together. Being separated from Lennox at this time must have brought fresh torment, she was having to grieve without him, as he was without her, the sooner he could leave Scotland and return to his wife the better for both of them.

Lennox continued in his plans to leave Scotland but before he departed, he rode to Stirling Castle to visit his 10-month-old grandson, he then waited for a ship to sail him back to England. He finally set sail on 29 April and arrived at anchor off the coast of Portsmouth on 10 May. Elizabeth granted him permission to come ashore and provided a passage of safe conduct for him to travel to London. But before Lennox could dock, his ship was blown by heavy winds across the channel and they had to take shelter in Brittany. These delays must have been agony for Margaret but he finally arrived in London on 12 June 1567, where husband and wife were reunited after three long years apart. They had both changed in those three years. Matthew's hair had gone white and he was showing signs of old age but more worryingly, his mental state seemed unstable and he was filled with hatred towards Mary and his son's killers to the point that he was borderline insane with rage. So much had happened in those three years, neither of them could have imagined how far they would go in their quest to put Darnley on the throne and the heartache they would face because of it. Now Lennox was home they could grieve, along with Charles, as a family and try to understand and come to terms with their loss.

Even though Lennox had left Scotland behind the council were still searching for justice, they were not fans of Darnley but neither did they appreciate Bothwell's attempts to seize power. Following the failure to bring him to trial, he seized control of the queen's person took control of Scotland. He intercepted her while she was travelling back to Edinburgh following a visit to her son in Stirling, from there he took her against her will Dunbar, where he allegedly held her prisoner and raped her. This version of events is often debated as many say the queen went with Bothwell of her own free will and the kidnap was staged by them both and because of it no one came to rescue her. In fact, there was no support coming for Mary from anywhere, England and Europe had turned a blind eye to what was happening and so she was left with no other option but to ally herself with Bothwell.

There had been many rumours flying around since the death of Darnley regarding the relationship between Mary and Bothwell, many accused them of plotting his murder together so they could marry. It was hoped the kidnap plot would help quash these rumours but when they married at Holyrood on 15 May 1567, she sealed her fate. She ought to have been in mourning for her late husband and yet there she was, remarrying just over three months later; she would maintain Bothwell had forced her into it, but it would become clear the affection ran both ways. More shocking revelations were to come when Mary announced she was pregnant by Bothwell, was this a marriage of love or necessity? Either way it condemned them both.

By June that year Mary had been overthrown. On 15 June at the battle of Carberry Hill, Mary and Bothwell's soldiers came face to face with those of the lords who opposed their marriage and who were seeking to avenge Darnley's death. The royal forces were soundly beaten, Bothwell managed to escape capture on the battlefield and when Mary offered to surrender on the proviso that Bothwell was given safe conduct out of Scotland, the lords agreed to let him go. Surely this was an act of love – Mary would not have wanted to aid a man who had supposedly kidnapped and raped her; if those claims had been true then this would provide Mary with an opportunity to rid herself of Bothwell.

Bothwell managed to escape to Denmark where he was later arrested and put in prison while Mary was to suffer the ultimate humiliation of being paraded through the streets of Edinburgh in utter shame, she was then taken to Loch Levan as a prisoner. During her imprisonment she gave birth to stillborn twins and while she was recovering from that ordeal, she was forced to abdicate her throne in favour of her 13-month-old son James; he was crowned just five days later at Stirling Castle. Mary's half-brother Moray was named regent, and Elizabeth urged her to make peace with him for he had been good to her. Mary's response to Elizabeth was that she was 'to meddle no further with private causes concerning him or any other subjects of Scotland'. Mary was telling Elizabeth to mind her own business but there was one Scottish subject they did have an interest in and that was the young king. The English would have preferred the boy to be sent to England and brought up by his grandparents in preparation for inheriting the throne, but with the regency now settled that was not a viable option.

The murder of Darnley is still hotly debated among historians today, many are ready to condemn Mary for her role in the plot and when faced with the evidence it is difficult to deny her guilt or defend her. However, an important question to answer is this: was the explosion intended to kill the queen as well? Many knew she was visiting her ill husband and may have seen it as an opportunity to rid themselves of both of them. If this is the case then the finger of blame must point towards Mary's enemies, which would mainly have been the Protestant faction in Scotland at the time, led by her own half-brother Moray. Mary did not return to the house again that night and Darnley managed to escape the blast, so were they tipped off that the gunpowder had been laid and they were the targets? Quite possibly. Many accuse Mary of not returning because she had ordered the explosion, but what if she hadn't? What if she was the intended target? We will never know the exact truth of what happened that night but it is unfair to lay the blame solely at Mary's feet without considering what was going on in the country at that time. She had never been a popular queen given her gender and religion, and marrying Darnley was an unpopular move so it is not a stretch to consider that the queen was a target too. If we consider that Mary was part of the plot then what where her motives? Darnley may have been an embarrassment to his wife but was that enough for her to kill him? Her councillors would have agreed to a divorce given their desire to rid the country of him, and he had such a lack of support that it would probably have been unchallenged. The accusations of adultery and violence could have persuaded the Pope to grant Mary her divorce, but given she was a Catholic she may have not seen this as an acceptable course of action – but then murder is not looked upon favourably either. I think one thing that can be agreed upon is that Bothwell probably arranged for the explosion; whether Mary was complicit too we simply do not know.

You cannot have an in-depth discussion about Margaret's life without taking a microscopic look at the life of Lord Darnley. He was the embodiment of everything Margaret wanted to achieve in her life. Once she understood the crown would never be hers, she lived her dreams through him and to see that come to such a brutal end was catastrophic. The Lennoxes mourned deeply for their son, but they knew that in their grandson James, their dreams were still alive.

You could say that Darnley deserved everything he got given his behaviour, his cruelness and petulance, his rudeness and arrogance which made his wife's life extremely difficult. In essence, Mary sacrificed her crown for Darnley, she just did not realise it at the time. But should we be so harsh on Darnley? Was he simply not just a product of his parents' desire? A young man who had grown up expecting at the very least to wear a crown, it is little wonder he became childlike when he did not get what he thought was rightly his. His descent into alcoholism and brutality was not surprising, he was surrounded by people that either despised him or bowed to his every whim; what he needed was a father who could place a firm hand on his shoulder and speak to him of propriety and decency. Whether Margaret was fully aware of her son's behaviour we do not know, but I think it is safe to assume Lennox would more than likely protect his wife from the worst of it.

Chapter 16

The Arrival of Mary, Queen of Scots, in England

It had been a difficult time for Margaret and Lennox, they had endured a three-year separation, imprisonment, and the murder of their eldest son. The worry about the safety of her husband and whether her grandson was secure on his throne had exhausted Margaret. Money was still a cause for concern despite being given some of their estates back, much of their land had been sold off which vastly reduced their rental income. However, they were determined that their son should be remembered so they commissioned Livinus de Vogelarre to paint a Memorial of Lord Darnley, which they dedicated to James. The oil painting depicts Darnley in his tomb with the black clad figures of Lennox, Margaret and Charles all praying behind the small, illuminated figure of Darnley's son, King James VI. On the side of the tomb are illustrative panels; one shows Darnley's body being dragged from his bed and the other shows his and his valet's body lying in the orchard. Also depicted in the bottom left-hand corner is the defeat of Mary's forces at Carberry Hill, it shows the queen surrendering herself to the lords who supported the Lennox family. Bothwell is seen cowardly riding away to the safety that exile afforded him. This painting is a powerful piece and anyone viewing it can be left in no doubt the Lennoxes held Mary responsible for Darnley's murder. It is believed the inscriptions written regarding Mary's involvement in her husband's death were removed by James at a later date. The painting is an impressive piece of propaganda and is there to remind people of the links between the Lennoxes and Scottish royalty, the young king was the one bright light to emerge from the disaster and they would do anything to preserve and uphold his right to rule.

Margaret and Lennox were convinced Mary was aware of the plot to murder their son and held her personally responsible for the tragedy, they were adamant she should never regain her throne. When she escaped from Loch Levan in May 1568, they were worried her remaining supporters would rally to her cause and reinstate her, usurping their grandson in the process. After a disastrous campaign to regain control Mary fled over the border into England in the hope that her cousin Elizabeth would offer her the support needed to regain control in Scotland. Mary's appearance in England alarmed the Lennoxes and they urged Elizabeth not to allow her to join the court, their main concern was that Mary would be able to charm Elizabeth into offering English support to unseat James in her favour. Elizabeth was a vain woman and was never going to allow another crowned queen to grace her court, especially one who was famed for her beauty. Instead, it was agreed the Scottish queen was to be taken to Carlisle Castle where she was placed into custody for her own protection.

Now she was in England, Margaret and Lennox wanted Mary to stand trial accused of the murder of Darnley, but Elizabeth was reluctant to take this course of action against an anointed queen without concrete evidence. Elizabeth may have had her doubts about Mary's innocence but that was not enough for her to agree to a trial, for all Mary's faults she was still a queen and Elizabeth held that in the highest regard. In order to placate the Lennoxes however, she offered them her full support in tracking down the culprits in Scotland and when Cecil approached Margaret to help him track down the remaining supporters of Bothwell, she was more than willing to oblige.

Mary being in England caused Elizabeth major problems; in the first instance she simply did not know what to do with her – should she keep her as prisoner or send her home to face her fate there? One thing she could not do was supply her with forces to regain her throne just in case she decided to turn them on her in a bid to claim the English throne instead. Religion was once again to become a factor. Mary, as a Catholic, could potentially become a figurehead for a rebellion in England so giving her back her freedom was not an option, and while Margaret was also a Catholic, the chances of her helping Mary were non-existent. Much to the relief of the Lennoxes it was agreed that bringing Mary to court was not an option either, she stood accused of being part of a plot to murder her husband and even though they were kinswomen Elizabeth also had an obligation to the welfare of her cousin Margaret. In Europe, Mary was widely considered to have been complicit in the plot to kill Darnley and Elizabeth could not be seen to condone this; despite the family connections, she had to remain neutral and so was left with no option but to keep Mary under house arrest. From Carlisle Castle, Mary was sent to Bolton Castle and that marked the start of her incarceration, she had swapped a Scottish prison for an English one.

Margaret did not have to wait long for evidence to appear that could see Mary put on trial. There had been a fortunate discovery in Scotland of a silver casket of letters that were reportedly written between Mary and Bothwell. The casket contained eight letters and sonnets dated between January and April 1567 and were seen as proof that Mary and Bothwell had concocted the plan to murder Darnley together. Mary denied ever having written the letters and claimed them to be forgeries, there were suggestions they had been written by Mary Beaton, one of her ladies in waiting. Regardless of this they were taken seriously by those who wished to see Mary punished for her role in the murder. In September 1568 the letters were brought to York by Regent Moray where the Duke of Norfolk was to preside over an inquiry to assess to what extent Mary was involved in the murder, he forwarded copies to Elizabeth and the Privy Council for them to assess. The letters were studied in minute detail, with samples of handwriting taken from Mary to compare, but the authenticity of the letters was questionable and a verdict of 'nothing proven' was reached, at which point the inquest was deferred to a panel in Westminster. Moray once again produced the letters at a hearing on 7 December and on 10 December he, along with other Scottish dignitaries, signed a deed confirming the letters had been written in Mary's own hand. On 14 December a further meeting was held at Hampton Court at which members of the Privy Council compared other examples of Mary's known handwriting to the letters. Once again, a verdict of not proven was reached, the English councillors believed the letters to be genuine but Elizabeth did not want to openly accuse or deny Mary's guilt and decided an open verdict would be best. The passing of this verdict protected Elizabeth from having to come face to face with Mary and also justified keeping her prisoner, which was no doubt good news for Margaret.

Mary refused to acknowledge the legitimacy of the inquest; she had not been permitted to attend the hearings in London but as an anointed queen and not being an English subject, she felt she could not be tried under English law, especially as the crime had taken place outside of England. Mary's supporters argued it had no place to be heard in an English court or to be presided over by English peers, those representing Mary felt there had been some kind of conspiracy to bring her character into further question. Mary remained in custody under the watchful eyes of the Earl of Shrewsbury and was moved among his residences until her final arrest in 1586, at which time she was moved to Fotheringhay Castle in Suffolk. This final arrest came on 15 August 1586 after Mary was implicated in a plot to assassinate Queen Elizabeth. The Babington Plot was a plan to encourage the Catholic forces of Spain and France to invade England to remove the Protestant Elizabeth in favour of the Catholic Mary. It was headed by Anthony Babington, an English gentleman, and John Ballard, a Jesuit priest. Thinking they had a band of loyal men all united in the cause of bringing England back into the Catholic church the men set about making contact with Mary. Unfortunately for them the others in the group were actually working for Elizabeth's secretary Francis Walsingham, and when encrypted letters between Mary and Babington were discovered in the cork of a beer barrel the plot unravelled. In October 1586 Mary went on trial for her role in the Babington Plot, she denied all knowledge of the plans but was found guilty and sentenced to death.

Elizabeth waivered and did not readily sign the death warrant, it would take until the following February for her to do so and even then, she did not set a date for the execution. Instead, Cecil gathered ten of the most trusted members of the Privy Council and without her knowledge arranged for the execution to be carried out immediately. Mary, Queen of Scots was finally executed on the morning of 8 February 1587; the executioner failed to remove her head with a single blow, instead it took several attempts to finally sever her head from her body. She was buried in Peterborough Cathedral, although in 1612 King James requested she be moved and reinterred in a vault in Westminster Abbey, taking her rightful place alongside many of her forebears and descendants. Mary was forty-four years old when she died and had lived nearly twenty years of her life as Elizabeth's prisoner.

Following Mary's trial of December 1568 for Darnley's murder, Margaret and Lennox did at last have some sort of closure; even though she had not been proven guilty or innocent, it was enough for them to finally move on. They were given leave by Elizabeth to return to their Yorkshire estates with their only surviving child for a period of solitude and reflection. They had suffered tragedy and loss but also triumph and they needed time to reflect and decide what their next move would be. One thing for certain was that all their efforts would go into the preservation of their grandson, King James VI of Scotland. They pleaded with Elizabeth to step in on their behalf to bring him to England, his safety was to be guaranteed at all costs, they were even willing to relocate to Scotland to be near him but the constant worry was starting to affect Lennox and Margaret was concerned that her husband was having a mental breakdown. Lennox had convinced himself that James would die at the hands of the Scottish lords and the angst and worry was inflamed even further when news reached England that Regent Moray had been assassinated at Linlithgow in January 1570 by a supporter of Mary called James Hamilton of Bothwellhaugh. Hamilton shot Moray from an upper window of the house of his uncle, Archbishop Hamilton, as the regent passed in the street below.

Chapter 17

The Assassination of Lennox

Moray had been a positive influence on the young king, he had been a stable and competent protector and had brought some stability to Scotland. Now he was dead, Margaret worried what was to become of her grandson. She wrote to Elizabeth to remind her of her promise to help the young king and requested again that he be brought to England for his own safety. In order to apply steady pressure on Elizabeth the Lennoxes relocated back to London, they took up residence at Somerset Place and petitioned the queen daily to bring James south to England. Elizabeth may have felt slightly uneasy at the prospect of having both the Scottish queen and her son the king in her realm at the same time. England had experienced a peaceful period and the last thing Elizabeth wanted to do was to create an air of unease. While she sympathised with the Lennoxes she was not willing to get involved.

The Scottish lords had their own agenda which included bringing Lennox north to be regent for his grandson but it was not a universally approved plan and there were factions in Scotland that opposed this idea. The Clan Hamilton wanted the restoration of the queen and felt that Lennox would be too impartial; he was the king's grandfather and despised Mary so would naturally come down hard on any supporters of the disgraced queen. From Elizabeth's point of view, she agreed with Hamilton's logic to a certain extent, her opinion was that the regent should be someone of a neutral background, one who could reason with both sides and with the capability of bringing peace and order to the country. Lennox, in her mind, was not the man for the job. For the first time in years England did not want to involve itself in Scotland's politics, the situation was too finely balanced and as

Elizabeth was already holding the queen there was a reluctance to be drawn in any further.

In April 1570 Elizabeth agreed that Lennox could leave England and travel back to Scotland. Once again Margaret bid her husband farewell, but like the trip with Darnley it was deemed necessary, except rather than putting a son on a throne, they had to keep their grandson on it. Lennox's presence in Scotland was paramount to ensure the safety of James and this made Margaret very matter of fact about the latest separation. While Lennox was away, Margaret stayed at court with Charles and anxiously awaited news of her husband's progress.

News came quickly and it was not good. Lennox was at Berwick when he had taken ill with a fever, it was so severe many thought him to be on his deathbed, a fact he wanted hidden from Margaret in order to spare her unnecessary worry. Thankfully he fully recovered and made his entrance into Edinburgh on 13 May, from there he rode on to Stirling arriving a few days later. In the early days things appeared to be going well; by June he was made Lieutenant of Scotland and was given full military command of the country's troops and only a matter of weeks later he was officially proclaimed regent, he was sworn in on 17 July 1570. James was being raised in the care of the Earl and Countess of Mar at Stirling Castle; they took care of the young child's immediate needs while his tutors took care of his education. He had been raised in the Protestant faith and Lennox made no attempt to change this – no doubt much to Margaret's dismay, but she could not win every battle. Elizabeth saw there were some positives to Lennox's appointment, she felt that having him in such a powerful role meant England's interests in Scotland were protected and she could look forward to a peaceful alliance at long last.

Elizabeth may have accepted the appointment of Lennox as regent but he was too pro-English to be wholly accepted by the Scots. There were many who were deeply unsatisfied with his appointment, mainly his old enemies the Clan Hamilton, and they were soon plotting his downfall. David Hamilton planned to capture Lennox while he travelled to Stirling, luckily the regent got wind of the plot and was ready for the ambush, he arranged for thirty men to be hanged for their involvement. Despite James having been crowned there were still supporters of Queen Mary who hankered after her restoration, they called themselves the Marian Party and they held both Dumbarton Castle and Edinburgh Castle in her name, making it difficult for Lennox to assert any real control. Things were not improving, he managed to lead a force to recapture Dumbarton Castle but without Edinburgh in his control, he found that he was becoming more isolated and at risk of further attack. The decision was made to retreat to the safety of Stirling where he was able to spend time with James. Lennox was a doting grandfather and developed a close bond with the young king and was with him in September 1571 at the state opening of parliament. Despite his good relationship with James his presence in Scotland was a great cause for concern for too many and on 4 September it all came to a tragic conclusion.

Lennox was struggling to find friends in Scotland; he soon found himself even more isolated than before and, in his frustration, began to become angry and unstable. The news worried Elizabeth enough to engage the services of the Earl of Sussex, Lord President of the North. She asked him to visit Scotland to talk to Lennox to see what was happening and to try and calm him down before he did something he would later have cause to regret. But Lennox didn't listen. Instead he captured John Hamilton, Archbishop of St Andrews, and put him on trial for his involvement in the murders of Darnley and Moray, at which he was found guilty; he was executed at Stirling on 6 April 1571. This proved to be a bad move by Lennox and by the summer his influence in Scotland was at an all-time low. By September, Queen Mary's supporters had had enough of the 'English Regent' and plans were soon being made to take action, led by George Gordon, 5th Earl of Huntley and Claud Hamilton, nephew to the executed Archbishop; they made the decision to oust Lennox from his role as regent. They marched towards Stirling with just one aim in mind, to remove Lennox from power at whatever cost. Lennox was staying at a house on the market square when at 4.00am he was rudely awoken by sounds of a skirmish.

The rebels' plan had been to take all prisoners back to Edinburgh alive but somewhere along the way the plan went wrong and Lennox, along with a small group of supporters, manged to escape and flee through the narrow streets of Stirling. Lennox was soon discovered by Captain James Calder and he followed the orders given by Huntly and Hamilton and shot Lennox. His single shot managed to hit Lennox in the lower stomach region, he was fatally wounded but somehow managed to stay on his horse and ride back to the castle. Sadly, the troops from the castle were too late and sixteen of Lennox's men were killed in the ensuing attack. Arriving back at the castle Lennox was helped from his horse by his servants who carried him through to the great hall, passing the young king on his way to his chamber, goodness knows what impact this had on the young boy but it must have been terrifying to see his grandfather so badly injured. A doctor was called but it was all in vain as it was quite clear Lennox was dying from his injuries. His first thought was the safety of his grandson the king, claiming 'if the bairn's well, all is well', he had literally given his life for the safety of the king and now, as the end neared, his protection remained at the forefront of Lennox's mind. Despite being in severe pain, on his deathbed Lennox forgave his enemies and pleaded with the lords that surrounded him to take care of the king, he must remain on the throne at all costs.

As Lennox prepared for death his final thoughts turned to Margaret, his wife of 26 years, the mother of his children and his most loyal supporter. It may have been a politically motivated marriage but it had also been one of deep love and respect, they had spent many years apart but both had worked tirelessly to bring about the advancement of their son and grandson. Matthew Stewart, Earl of Lennox, died at 4.00pm on 4 September 1571 at the age of fifty-four. At the age of fifty-six Margaret was now a widow. Having lost all but one of her eight children she had now lost her beloved husband, all in the pursuit of greatness. When confirmation of his death reached Cecil, it was agreed Elizabeth would break the news to her cousin, naturally she was devastated and was inconsolable, how would she ever be able to come to terms with this latest loss. Lennox was buried at the Chapel Royal at Stirling Castle, where Margaret would later erect a memorial to him.

Lennox was a man who was called upon in times of trouble, both England and Scotland used him to their own advantages and yet he never really enjoyed success in any of the aims he set out to achieve. His childhood had been traumatic and he spent much of his early adult years at odds with either the Scottish or the English until he married his love, Margaret Douglas. He saw his son and grandson sit on the throne of Scotland only to see Darnley murdered and James left vulnerable at the hands of men who sought their own advancement. He tried his best to bring peace to Scotland and had he been given more time and support he may well have achieved it, but it was a thankless task. Scotland was a country constantly at odds with itself, and whoever took on the role of regent could never hope to satisfy a council of ministers whose loyalties shifted. As regent to his grandson, Lennox could have ruled over Scotland, maybe with Margaret at his side, and see the country prosper under his governance and be at peace with itself. But alas, for the third time in as many years, Scotland was looking to appoint a new regent.

The Earl of Mar was proclaimed regent on 5 September 1571 but his appointment brought no peace and the Marian faction continued to oppose the rule of the king. The last few remaining supporters of Lennox vowed to get revenge for his murder. Initially, there was some confusion over who had fired the fatal shot, some even insinuated it was one of Lennox's own men who had shot in panic, but Captain Calder and his accomplices admitted their part in the regent's assignation, insisting they were only following orders. Mar ordered the execution of Calder; he died an agonising death ten days later. Mar would not fare much better; he died in in Stirling on 29 October 1572 following a short illness that some attributed to poisoning.

Margaret struggled to make sense of Lennox's death. She had been riding high at court, she was in favour with Elizabeth, who seemed to value the opinion of her older cousin, but with the appointment of Mar as regent her hopes of being involved with the upbringing of her grandson seemed as far away as they ever had done. But Margaret was never a woman to be defeated or to let her grief consume her and while her grandson sat on the throne of Scotland, she still had a purpose. Her dream of a United Kingdom of England and Scotland was still very much a reality, but the harsh truth was she had no access to James and now she had lost her husband, she faced an uncertain future.

Chapter 18

Plotting with Bess of Hardwick

By 1572 Charles Stewart was 15 years old and had suffered the loss of his elder brother and father in the most violent of ways. At times he seemed to be an afterthought, but now he was the remaining son and heir to the Lennox lands. Up to this point, Charles has been a figure that loomed in the background of Margaret's story, he was too young to be given a voice during his parents' troubles and being over ten years younger than Darnley, he had been a young boy when Darnley married Mary. But with his father and brother dead, the focus was on him; by rights he ought to have been regarded as a person of some importance as he shared the same royal Tudor blood as Darnley and was therefore was a claimant to the English throne.

At fifteen he was an out-of-control teenager – who could blame him for going off the rails considering what he had experienced so far in life? Margaret needed to rein in her youngest son before he did something reckless. The time had come for him to begin his formal education and Margaret once again turned for guidance to her old friend Cecil, who was created Lord Burghley in 1571, as Master of the Court of Wards. Ordinarily, when the father of a young noble child passed away, they would be given over to the court as wards, the guardianship would then be passed over to a wealthy man of means who would look to their upbringing and education. However, it appears that Charles was granted permission to stay in the care of his mother, this was more than likely granted by Elizabeth as an act of compassion. Burghley suggested Margaret seek the services of Swiss tutor Peter Malliet, and Charles was subsequently sent to live with him at his home in Gray's Inn where he was educated and brought up in a manner that would befit a man of his station. Much to Margaret's

153

relief Charles settled well and flourished under Malliet's guidance. While Charles was still a minor, Elizabeth permitted Margaret to collect the rent that was due from the properties Henry VIII had given her at the time of her marriage which helped to ease her financial burden. But news soon reached Margaret that the earldom of Lennox had merged with the crown, meaning James was the next Earl of Lennox following his grandfather's death, which took the title, and revenues, away from Charles. The Earl of Mar agreed with Margaret that Charles should be the next recipient of the Lennox earldom and agreed to look into the matter on her behalf. He was successful and Charles was declared Earl of Lennox in April, albeit in a new creation of the title.

With Charles's future now more stable and with a regular source of income Margaret retired to her Yorkshire estates for a quiet life, but her solitude would not last long. She was seen as too powerful a figure in both realms to be allowed to slip away to the Yorkshire countryside for too long. This was a fact acknowledged by the new regent, James Douglas, Earl of Morton. Sadly, when Mar died on 29 October 1572 at Stirling Castle following a short illness, the decision had been made to place the guardianship of the king with four nobles; Morton understood that as the king's grandmother Margaret held sway and could not – should not – be barred from his upbringing. But there was yet more trouble brewing. Mary's supporters still had control of Edinburgh and while they did the country could not settle into peace. Elizabeth sent her forces north of the border to finally put an end to their rebellion and in the spring of 1573 the Edinburgh castle fell to the king's men and some kind of order was restored. There was never any realistic chance that Mary could return to rule Scotland, the idea of a joint rule between her and James was suggested but in reality, it was never given too much credence.

Margaret had maintained her animosity towards Mary, still believing she was in some way responsible for her son's death. Surprisingly, that was going to change in 1575 when Margaret read a handwritten account from Bothwell that stated Mary was not involved in any way with Darnley's death and the blame was all his and his supporters. The authenticity of this account is somewhat questionable, given that it was supposedly written from his deathbed at Malmo Castle, Denmark when in fact he had left there for Dragsholm Castle in 1573 where he would die in 1578. The supposed witness to his confession had also been dead for some time. Nonetheless, Margaret took it as a true account and was finally reconciled with her daughter-in-law. After all, they did have one common interest – the welfare of the young king. Mary had never stopped enquiring after her son, despite him being taught to despise his mother; her love for him was unwavering and with a reconciliation with Margaret a new line of communication opened up which brought the captive queen fresh hope. As a token of love for her daughter-in-law Margaret sent Mary a 'point tresse', a lace embroidery made from her own greying hair. Mary would treasure this token for the remainder of her life

Margaret did not remain in Yorkshire long. She still had a son with royal blood, one who had interests in the English and Scottish thrones and would be in want of a wife; not one to let an advantageous opportunity go by she began to plot Charles's future. Margaret entered into a risky plot with one of the country's most influential women: the formidable Bess of Hardwick, Countess of Shrewsbury, whose daughter, Elizabeth Cavendish, needed a husband. Bess's husband had been gaoler to Mary, Queen of Scots for many years and it is likely the queen knew of the plot to marry the young couple as she had formed a close bond with Elizabeth. Bess and Margaret were of a similar outlook and standing; although Bess did not have the royal status Margaret had, she did have immense wealth, power and respect. Both women were ambitious and the advancement of their children was paramount to them; Bess had amassed a considerable fortune from her previous marriages which would have been a huge incentive for Margaret. For Bess, Charles was uncle to a king and the possibility of him becoming one himself one day could not be passed over lightly.

Buoyed by these prospects the women entered into negotiations about how they could bring the match about. They were aided by another influential woman of good standing, Katherine Willoughby, Duchess of Suffolk. Charles was a member of the royal family and it would have been considered treason for him to marry without his monarch's prior consent, but Margaret had clearly not learned any lessons from her previous marriage negotiations and once again she failed to get permission from Elizabeth before embarking on her plans. Unlike his brother at the time of his marriage, Charles was a resident of England and was marrying a fellow English subject; whereas Darnley had been protected in Scotland from any punishment Elizabeth could exact on him, Margaret was exposing Charles to danger. He could face imprisonment in the Tower – or worse, it seems incredulous that Margaret would bargain the liberty of her son like this given he was all she had left. She must have been confident that when Elizabeth eventually found out she would be lenient towards her son and instead take her anger out on her.

Knowing she would probably have forbidden the match the two women decided to press ahead without her blessing, their plans would have to be watertight and meticulously plotted in advance if they were going to pull this off. Margaret had loved and lost; she had seen her first love Thomas Howard perish in the Tower, and her beloved husband die at the hands of assassins, while Darnley was forced into a loveless marriage in the pursuit of power and glory. The least she could do was let Charles marry for love.

The marriage between Katherine Grey and the Earl of Hertford had been annulled in 1562 and their children declared illegitimate and it was apparent that Elizabeth was never going to marry and have children of her own which meant King James was next in line for the throne of England. It was felt by the Privy Council that the young king should be brought to England to be raised at court in preparation for his kingship. Margaret backed this plan wholeheartedly and Elizabeth granted her permission to travel north with Charles in a bid to put pressure on the Scots to relinquish their authority over him. She also unwittingly granted permission for Margaret to visit Bess as long as she did not visit her at Chatsworth or go within thirty miles of Sheffield Castle, she did not want to risk any chance of Margaret and Mary coming together while she was on her way north. If the queen had any suspicions a plot was afoot, it would have been unlikely for her to have granted permission for Margaret and Bess to meet.

Margaret and Charles left London in October with the plan to marry Charles to Elizabeth already agreed, although it is unsure if he was aware of the plans as they headed north. While en route they were advised that the Scots had no intention of giving their young king over to the English and there was no point in them continuing any further. Disappointed at this latest development, Margaret decided to stop at Grimsthorpe Castle in Lincolnshire to rest. Rather coincidently, this just so happened to be one of the Duchess of Suffolk's properties and made for a convenient stopping point to go and meet Bess, who was staying at the nearby Rufford Abbey. On the face of it this was just a happy coincidence, but in fact it had been planned perfectly and gave the two ladies an opportunity to discuss the finer points of the marriage contract.

During her stay, Margaret fell ill and Bess kindly offered to take care of her friend, leaving the two youngsters an opportunity to get to know each other by themselves and by all accounts they fell in love with each other almost immediately. Their mothers might have connived to bring about this meeting, but it was down to Charles and Elizabeth to do the rest and they did not waste any time in declaring their love for each other. After telling their mothers they had fallen in love, they were married on 5 November in the chapel at Rufford Abbey. It appears the queen was not the only person not to have been informed of the plans, the Earl of Shrewsbury only found out about his stepdaughter's marriage after it had occurred, and despite being pleased with the match, he was unable to provide her with a dowry at such short notice. Bess of Hardwick was a formidable woman, rather like Margaret, they were cut from the same cloth and both had the ability to coerce their husbands into changing their minds. Shrewsbury managed to provide a dowry of £3,000 and Bess offered Margaret loans to help with her finances. They may have negotiated Shrewsbury, but they still had to face the reaction from Elizabeth, neither knew how she would react but they could probably hazard a guess that it was not going to be favourable – and they were right.

Elizabeth was apoplectic with rage when she heard of the young lovers' nuptials. After finally reconciling the succession on James, the actions of these two young lovers could turn everything on its head. Had Margaret not realised that should Charles and Elizabeth have a son it could potentially displace James as the English heir? Their child would be an English subject and would therefore supplant any Scottish-born heir, there would be no uniting of the thrones so had Margaret thrown away her dream of unification? Or had she astutely realised she could potentially have a grandson sat on each throne, both ruling their own country in their own right.

Just over a month after leaving, Margaret, Charles and his new bride Elizabeth were summoned back to London to explain their reckless actions. Their journey was not easy, the weather had turned to sleet and thunderstorms and it took them until 10 December to arrive, all the while giving Elizabeth time to get angrier. Margaret had upset her yet again and needed help so she turned the Earl of Leicester, hoping he could once again calm the queen and make her listen to reason, he obliged Margaret again but even he could not calm Elizabeth down. Upon their arrival Margaret was sent to her home at Hackney where she was placed under house arrest, Charles and Elizabeth were separated while an investigation took place. Margaret and Shrewsbury appealed to the queen, explaining it was an innocent love affair that had gone too far before it could be stopped, a wedding was the only option left to them if they were to save his stepdaughter from ruin.

Margaret pleaded with Elizabeth; she reminded her she had followed orders and kept away from Mary, but Bess's closeness to the Scottish queen put Elizabeth on high alert. In her mind this was another plot by Catholics to oust her from her throne, after all those years she still believed there was a European-wide network of spies all working together to depose her and place a Catholic monarch on the English throne. Margaret's explanation to the queen was that the meeting between Charles and Elizabeth, and her illness during the trip, were all beyond Margaret's control; they were all victims of circumstance and there was nothing she could do to prevent it. It all sounded plausible – until Shrewsbury confessed that the marriage had been in the works for over a year. This had become serious. This was treason.

Chapter 19

Margaret's Final Years

On 27 December 1574 Margaret returned to the Tower of London for the third time as a prisoner, once again she had forfeited her land and income to the crown. A full investigation was ordered by Elizabeth and she tasked Francis Walsingham in leading the inquest, he in turn appointed Henry Hastings, Earl of Huntingdon, to question Margaret and Bess, who by now had been placed under house arrest at Rufford Abbey. Despite Shrewsbury and Leicester appealing on her behalf, in Elizabeth's eyes this was all Margaret's doing and she was going to be the one to suffer for it. She was convinced there was a much wider plot to remove her from the throne but the investigation showed no evidence of this, in fact it showed nothing that could be deemed treasonable.

The official conclusion was that Charles and the young Elizabeth had met by chance and fallen in love, and that Queen Elizabeth had overreacted. They had got away with it and Margaret was released from the Tower and cleared of all charges. Elizabeth gave birth to hers and Charles baby, a daughter they named Arbella. Queen Mary stood as godmother to her niece and the happy family were soon comfortably ensconced at Hackney with Margaret, who after so much personal loss and grief finally had a grandchild she could hold in her arms and dote on. But in a final cruel twist of fate the happiness was to be short lived. Charles contracted tuberculosis and died in April 1576 at the age of just 19, leaving Elizabeth a widow and baby Arbella fatherless. He was temporarily laid to rest at St Augustine's church in Hackney, although Margaret had made plans for her own tomb in Westminster Abbey in which he would join her when the time came. Margaret had outlived her husband and all her children and faced old age alone and in poverty.

With Charles gone the focus of Margaret's life was her baby granddaughter and her advancement, it was Margaret's view that Arbella should inherit the title of Countess of Lennox from her father, but James kept the title and revenues for himself, although he later bestowed it on the Bishop of Caithness, who was Charles's uncle. It was quite clear they wanted to keep the money in Scotland rather than let the rightful, English, heiress inherit. Margaret found herself trying to appease her grandson hoping he would look kindly on his cousin but it was felt that Arbella was too young to inherit the title and Morton argued that it should revert to the crown until she came of age. The loss of income in her old age would be felt dearly by Margaret, even Queen Elizabeth tried to intervene on her behalf, and Mary added a codicil to her will that when she died the title and lands should pass to Arbella. Sadly, as Mary was no longer the reigning queen she no longer had the right to make such requests and her demand was overlooked. In the end, Morton had the title made extinct and it reverted back to the crown.

Burghley granted the wardship of Arbella to Margaret but the decision was made for the baby and her mother to return to Bess at Hardwick Hall where Arbella would spend the majority of her childhood. She was first cousin to James and so, having a claim to the throne, she would remain a person of interest; a poisoned chalice no doubt and later she would follow in her grandmother's footsteps into the Tower of London after marrying without her cousin's consent.

In early 1578, Margaret made her will, the majority of her estate was left to Arbella, including all her jewels. James was bequeathed a black velvet bed that was embroidered with golden flowers, her longstanding friend Cecil was left a diamond ring and Dudley was left a large portrait of her beloved uncle, King Henry. There were also many charitable donations and gifts for her servants.

In mid-March she had dinner with her long-time friend the Earl of Leicester. Dudley had stepped in to help Margaret on many occasions; interceding with Elizabeth could not have been an easy task given the tensions between the two cousins but he was always willing to try. The evening after Leicester left Hackney, Margaret fell ill and took to her bed; she died peacefully on the evening of 10 March 1578 aged sixty-two. Many suspected Leicester of foul play but I do not subscribe to this theory, the two appeared to enjoy a close friendship and there was no reason for him to take such drastic action. If he had wanted to despatch Margaret, he would have done it years earlier, it made no sense for him to do it now when her health was already starting to fail her. It is more likely she suffered a stroke or heart attack. Her state of mind at the time of her death is open to debate; she had loved and lost countless times in her life, suffered years of imprisonment and had sunk to depths of poverty that a lady of her station should not have reached. While she had two grandchildren to dote on, she had little to no physical contact with them. She never met James, and following Arbella's move to the Midlands her involvement would have been reduced somewhat. After living a life as frenetic as she had it is reasonable to assume Margaret was tired of life and approached death as she did with any other obstacle she met in life – head on and full of strength.

Margaret was given a state funeral as was her right as cousin to the queen and as a granddaughter to a king, for Elizabeth to do anything less than this would have been seen as spiteful on her part. She was laid to rest at Westminster Abbey on 3 April 1578. Her funeral was a grand ceremony with many mourners. Her coffin was carried by eight gentlemen of the realm and behind them came the chief mourner Margaret Clifford, Countess of Derby, who led a group of noble women, one of them was Elizabeth Cavendish, Margaret's daughter-in-law, and Lettice Knollys, Countess of Essex and soon to be bride of Robert Dudley, Earl of Leicester. Heralds carried Margaret's arms showing her Scottish and English royal lineage. Once the Abbey was full the funeral could take place. Despite living and dying a Catholic, it was a Protestant service conducted by John Piers, Bishop of Salisbury. The Westminster Abbey website gives us a fascinating description of the ceremony:

the coffin was to be met at the west door by the ministers and choir and during the procession to the hearse 'I am the resurrection and the life' was to be said or sung. Two or three psalms are suggested and after the sermon there was the commemoration at the Communion Table with the epistle and gospel being read. At the offering some parts of Scripture were to be sung. The service then proceeded according to the prayer book.

She was finally fully laid to rest in October of 1578 after the tomb she had commissioned was finally completed. It was made of alabaster with the effigy of Margaret lying with her hands clasped together in prayer, she is shown wearing a countess's coronet and draped in a bright red cloak with an ermine trim over a gown of blue and gold with ruffs at her neck and cuffs. Along each side in a kneeling position are the eight children she had borne and lost, four daughters (whose names were not recorded) down one side and her four sons down the other, the Scottish crown sits suspended above the head of Darnley. In the centre of her sons is her coat of arms. On the panel the inscription reads: (the following translations have been taken from the Westminster Abbey website):

HEER LYETH THE NOBLE LADY MARGARET, COUNTESSE OF LEVENOX, DAUGHTER AND SOLE HEIRE OF ARCHIBALD EARLE OF ANGUISE [Angus], BY MARGARET Q. OF SCOTTES HIS WIFE THAT WAS ELDEST DAUGHTER TO KING HENRY THE 7, WHOE BARE UNTO MATHEW EARLE OF LEVENOX HER HUSBAND 4 SONNES AND 4 DAUGHTERS. THIS LADY HAD TO HER GREAT GRANDFATHER K.EDWARD THE 4, TO HER GRANDFATHER K.HENRY THE 7, TO HER UNCLE K.HENRY THE 8, TO HER COUSIN GERMANE K.EDWARD THE 6, TO HER BROTHER

K.JAMES OF SCOTLAND THE V, TO HER SONNE KING HENRY THE FIRST [i.e. Lord Darnley], TO HER GRANDCHILD K.JAMES THE 6. HAVINGE TO HER GREATE GRANDMOTHER AND GRANDMOTHER 2 QUEENES BOTH NAMED ELIZABETH, TO HER MOTHER MARGARET Q. OF SCOTTS, TO HER AUNT MARYE THE FRENCHE Q, TO HER COUSYNS GERMANES MARY AND ELIZABETH QUEENES OF ENGLAND, TO HER NEECE AND DAUGHTER IN LAW MARY Q. OF SCOTTS. HENRY SECOND SONNE TO THIS LADY WAS K. OF SCOTTS AND FATHER TO JAMES THE 6 NOW KING. THIS HENRY WAS MURTHERED AT THE AGE OF 21 YEARES. CHARLES HER YOUNGEST SONNE WAS EARLE OF LEVENOX FATHER TO THE LADIE ARBELL. HE DYED AT THE AGE OF 21 YEARES AND IS HERE INTOMBED.

The inscription on the western side of the tombs reads:

Sacred to the memory of MARGARET DOUGLAS, wife of Matthew Stuart, Earl of Lennox, granddaughter to Henry VII, King of England, by his daughter (Margaret Tudor): joined by the closest ties of kinship to most puissant kings, grandmother to James VI of Scotland, a lady of most pious character, invincible spirit, and matchless steadfastness. She died the tenth of March, year of Our Lord 1577. Margaret, mighty in virtue, mightier yet in lineage: ennobled by kings and by her forebears; descended from Scottish and English princes, she was also a progenitor of princes. Those things that belong unto death, she released to death most joyfully, and sought God, for she belonged to God before.

Charles was interred beside her following the completion of the tomb and Arbella lies at rest nearby, she died in 1615.

Margaret's tomb lies under the magnificent fan vaulted ceiling in the south aisle of the Lady Chapel close to her great-grandmother Margaret Beaufort. The chapel was built by her grandfather King Henry VII in memory of his queen, and her grandmother, Elizabeth of York.

Chapter 20

Margaret Douglas's Legacy

While writing this book it occurred to me on numerous occasions that by the standards of the day, Margaret was lucky, very lucky indeed. During her uncle's reign she endured imprisonment in the Tower of London, a building that drove fear into the heart of any Tudor courtier, if you entered there you very rarely left with your head attached to your shoulders. Henry was not known for his forgiving nature, once crossed it was unlikely you would ever return to favour, but somehow Margaret did, and did it twice. You could argue that this was simply because he did not want to execute his own blood, but he did not apply that logic when it came to Margaret Pole, Countess of Salisbury. She was the cousin of Henry's mother, Elizabeth of York, and endured a truly horrific execution when her head was literally hacked from her body. While Margaret was imprisoned for her affair with Thomas Howard, she was probably saved extreme punishment for her indiscretion with Charles Howard as Henry was dealing with a much bigger betrayal – that of his wife and queen, Catherine Howard.

So, was there something about Margaret Douglas that Henry felt specifically akin too? She was not even the daughter of his favourite sister Mary. Bar Prince Arthur, all the Tudor siblings had been brought up together in the nursery at Eltham Palace and a bond would have formed between them, Henry may have been at odds with his sister Margaret during their adult lives but she was still his beloved elder sister, how could he ever bring himself to face her again had he executed her daughter. Following her separate indiscretions with Thomas and Charles Howard, the king could have chosen to make an example of his niece, using her as a warning to all the other royal cousins that regardless of blood ties and closeness to the throne, if you cross uncle Henry then you will pay the ultimate price.

The truth of the matter is that Margaret and King Henry shared a close relationship, she was fond of him, and he clearly doted on her. From a young age he seems to have gone out of his way to ensure she was brought up in the manner that was due her rank, clothing, housing, feeding and educating her like a princess and to his own cost. He understood that the actions of her parents were in no way a reflection on her; she was young and innocent and caught up in a war that had little to do with her. There may have been fallings out, as in any family, but Henry respected his niece for her ability to believe in her own convictions, she was stubborn and headstrong, but then so was he.

Margaret offered Henry a close female family connection; he rarely saw his sisters – one was in Scotland and the other rarely visited court, and his relationship with his own daughters was strained due to his dealings with their mothers, but in Margaret he found an intelligent woman who he could admire. She had deftly negotiated the 'king's great matter' while still maintaining her friendship with Princess Mary, she was loyal to her friend while understanding the importance of courtly life and she understood her role within that. Margaret offered Henry a viable option as heir to his throne, hers was a claim that was, up until her dealing with Thomas Howard, unblemished. Mary and Elizabeth had been declared illegitimate, Henry Fitzroy was dead and before the birth of Prince Edward, Margaret must have been a realistic option, it must have certainly crossed Henry's mind. But was she ever really considered a viable option as monarch? Possibly, had Catholicism prevailed in England like it had in Spain then it is quite possible she may have maintained her place in the line of succession, but Henry's children were the rightful heirs, and it was right and proper they inherited the throne as per his will. Given everything that happened during Margaret's life it was unlikely she would have sat on the throne of England as queen unless it happened through conquest as her grandfather had done all those years before, and that would have required help from outside the country.

Her relationship with Elizabeth was often strained, they had never been close, there was a substantial age gap and her loyalties had always been with Mary so with Elizabeth as monarch she was going to have to watch her step. You would be forgiven for thinking that the horrors of the Tower of London would have been enough to refrain her from ever crossing her monarch's wrath again, but for Margaret that threat of danger did not seem to cloud her judgement when it came to decision making. She knew full well that negotiating her son's marriages without Elizabeth's consent was wrong and would place her at her mercy but she forged on regardless, the prizes were always much bigger than the punishment as far as she was concerned. The marriage of Darnley to Mary, Queen of Scots was a huge prize and to go as far as openly taking an oath agreeing to the exact opposite shows us a ruthless, and maybe even a reckless woman. Margaret never seemed to waiver over the proposed marriage, she does not appear to have ever considered the consequences of her actions for her or others. It is hard to believe she naively thought she would get away unpunished, but more likely she was willing to take the risk for the sake of her son, it is just a shame her son did not embrace the opportunity he had been given.

Elizabeth was well within her rights to imprison Margaret and seize her lands, although she had not necessarily plotted directly against Elizabeth, she had clearly plotted against the stability of the country and that was an act of treason, punishable by death. But, like her father, Elizabeth never charged or punished Margaret beyond imprisonment, and even then it was not always a harsh punishment given the relative comfort she enjoyed as a lady of rank. The biggest punishment for Margaret was the separation from her loved ones; while her son Darnley was living the life of a king in Scotland, she was languishing in the Tower unable to revel in his success. Without the support of her husband, Lennox, she also had to deal with the news that Darnley had been murdered, possibly on the orders of his wife. Separated from Lennox by so many miles in an age when news took days to filter through must have been more than she could bear, but bear it she did because Darnley's marriage had yielded her a grandson and future king.

Margaret had much to deal with in her life: she lost her beloved husband and all but one of her eight children so can she not be forgiven for wanting to advance him as much as she could? I think so; she would have known what she faced when her plotting was discovered, but as a mother she was willing to take that risk and pay the ultimate price if she had to. Having said that, she probably felt confident that Elizabeth would not unleash the full penalty on her, she had gotten away with it before so why not now?

Margaret Douglas, Countess of Lennox, lived a full life, carefully negotiating her way through Tudor life. As a Tudor, she never lost sight of her true value and standing and can be forgiven for entertaining ideas that one day she could rule. But that begs the question: did she ever actually see herself on the throne of England, or did those aspirations lie in her ambitions for her children? If she stood any chance at all, it was during the reign of Queen Mary; as a Catholic she would have wanted to pass her crown on to someone else of that religion but unfortunately the Privy Council just saw Margaret as a danger, they wanted the return of Protestantism and with that came Elizabeth. Margaret would have been well aware that with the death of Mary so went her chances of queenship; as Elizabeth ascended to her rightful place Margaret had no choice but to accept it and move her attentions elsewhere. As well as navigating the religious minefield that was Tudor England, Margaret also managed to balance the English and Scottish factions in her life, and showed resilience when taken from her home and brought to England. Even though she was disinherited by her father from the Angus estates and title, she tried to remain on relatively good terms with the regents and later Queen Mary, all the while juggling her relationship with Elizabeth. It was not an easy position to be in, all those years before, when Henry VII was negotiating for his daughter's marriage, little did he realise the impact it would have on the life of his granddaughter.

The role of mother was very important to Margaret. It is believed she gave birth to eight children although there are some who suggest she had nine, I am happy to accept it was eight given the decoration on her tomb. Sadly, we have no records regarding the exact dates or places of birth for her daughters or how long they lived which could suggest they died at birth, or very shortly after and certainly by early infancy. Margaret certainly fulfilled her duty as wife by providing Lennox with his heirs. She was a domineering mother and commanded the utmost respect from her children, which leads me to believe Darnley would have behaved differently had his mother been close at hand to guide him. Both boys appreciated her ability to read certain situations and they trusted her judgement when it came to their social advancement, both understanding that it was their advancement and happiness that mattered most to her. From the accounts of her devastation when she learned of their deaths, we can only assume the relationships she shared with Darnley and Charles were close and loving.

History seems to have forgotten Margaret Douglas. Other than being mentioned in books as Darnley's mother there is very little written about her but that is not to discredit her place among the Tudor royal family. She was an integral part of the reign of all but one Tudor monarch (that being her grandfather King Henry VII), she served princesses and queens and took her rightful place at the head of many a royal procession. Maybe if she had died at the hands of the executioner more people would be aware of who she was and the legacy she left behind. Her name would be taught in history classes today but instead, because she died in her bed from illness at the age of sixty-two, her reputation seems to have died with her; without Margaret Douglas the line of our royal families would look very different. Her importance in English and Scottish history should not be underestimated or overlooked for she was integral to life on both sides of the border.

Margaret's main aim was to see the unification of the thrones of England and Scotland, ideally under Catholic monarchs but even she could not do enough to stem the tide of Protestantism that swept both countries. Twenty-five years after her death however, and following the death of Queen Elizabeth I on 24 March 1603, her grandson King James VI of Scotland became King James I of England, marking the start of a new age. Tudor rule had come to an end and a Stuart era was about to begin. Had she lived to see James take the English throne no doubt she would have been a very proud grandmother. After the loss and heartache in her life it had all been worth it, her dream had finally come true and the role she played in bringing it about was instrumental. Her blood has run in the veins of every monarch since.

Bibliography

Armitage, J, *Four Queens and a Countess*, (Amberley, Stroud, 2019)

Borman, T, *The Private Lives of the Tudors: Uncovering the Secrets of Britain's Greatest Dynasty*, (Hodder & Stoughton, London, 2016)

Clegg, M, *Margaret Tudor: The Life of Henry VIII's Sister*, (Pen and Sword History, Barnsley, 2018)

Dunn, J, *Elizabeth & Mary, Cousins, Rivals, Queens,* (Harper Perennial, London, 2003)

Durant, D.N, *Bess of Hardwick: Portrait of an Elizabethan Dynast*, (Peter Owen Publishers, London, 2008)

Fraser, A, *Mary Queen of Scots*, (Phoenix Press, London, 2002)

Gristwood, S, *England's Lost Queen Arbella*, (Bantam Books, London, 2004)

Gristwood, S, *Elizabeth & Leicester*, (Transworld (Bantam Press), London, 2008)

Gristwood, S, *Game of Queens: The Women Who Made Sixteenth Century Europe*, (Oneworld, London, 2016)

Guy, J, *My Heart is My Own: The Life of Mary Queen of Scots*, (Fourth Estate, London, 2009)

Hubbard, K, *Devices & Desires: Bess of Hardwick and the Building of Elizabethan England*, (Vintage, London, 2019)

MacCulloch, D, *Thomas Cromwell, A Life*, (Penguin Random House, London, 2018)

Massie, A, *The Royal Stuarts* (Jonathan Cape, London, 2010).

Mayhew, M, *House of Tudor: A Grisly History*, (Pen & Sword History, Barnsley, 2022)

McGregor, M, *The Other Tudor Princess*, (The History Press, Stroud, 2016)

Porter, L, *Crown of Thistles: The Fatal Inheritance of Mary, Queen of Scots*, (PAN Books, London, 2014)

Ring, M, *So High a Blood*, (Bloomsbury, London, 2018)

Stedall, R, *Mary Queen of Scots' Downfall: The Life and Murder of Henry, Lord Darnley*, (Pen and Sword History, Barnsley, 2017)

Tallis, N, *Elizabeth's Rival: The Tumultuous Life of Lettice Knollys, Countess of Leicester*, (Michael O'Mara Books, London, 2018)

Weir, A, *Henry VIII: King and Court*, (Vintage, London, 2010)

Weir, A, *The Lost Princess: A Life of Margaret Douglas, Countess of Lennox*, (Jonathan Cape, London, 2015)

Whitelock, A, *Mary Tudor, England's First Queen*, (Bloomsbury, London, 2009)

Whitelock, A, *Elizabeth's Bedfellows: An Intimate History of the Queen's Court*, (Bloomsbury, 2013)

Wilkinson, J, *Catherine Howard: The Tragic Story of Henry VIII's Fifth Queen* (John Murray, London, 2017)

Williams, K, *Rival Queens, The Betrayal of Mary, Queen of Scots*, (Penguin Random House, London, 2018)

Online Resources

www.english-heritage.org.uk/visit/places/norham-castle/
www.harbottlecastle.co.uk
www.historicenvironment.scot/visit-a-place/places/linlithgow-palace/
www.rct.uk
www.trc-leiden.nl/trc-needles/individual-textiles-and-textile-types/daily-and-general-garments-and-textiles/the-lennox-point-tresse
www.westminster-abbey.org

Index